Margo,

With much love

Giuseppe

x

14 February 1996 .

GW00502551

Classic

Love Poems

SUMMERSDALE

Copyright © Summersdale Publishers 1995

All rights reserved.

No part of this book may be reproduced by any means, nor transmitted, nor translated into a machine language, without the written permission of the publisher.

Summersdale Publishers
46 West Street
Chichester
West Sussex
PO19 1RP
United Kingdom

A CIP catalogue record for this book is available from the British Library.

Printed and bound in Great Britain
by Selwood Printing Ltd., Burgess Hill.

ISBN 1 873475 51 9

Cover illustration courtesy of The Fine Art Photographic Library Ltd., London.

Illustrations by Sophie Sitwell.

Classic Love Poems was originally published in hardback 1994.

*This book is dedicated
to the memory of Arif Kus.*

Contents

Introduction

Of all the stimuli that have inspired poets over the centuries, love in all its guises has been an unceasingly rich and varied source of powerful, romantic and exquisite verse.

Love poems have retained their popularity through the years by expressing eternal and universal emotions. We have all been struck by the sheer force of love when it hits: as Chaucer describes it in *The Knight's Tale,*

> "He cast his eye upon Emelya,
> And therwithal he bleynte and cride, "A!"
> As though he stongen were unto the herte."

This account of pure, elevated love is typical of the tone adopted by many of the poets. In *Doctor Faustus,* Marlowe gives us possibly some of the most beautiful lines ever written in the English language, in praise of Helen of Troy,

> "Was this the face that launched a thousand ships
> And burnt the topless towers of Ilium?
> Sweet Helen, make me immortal with a kiss."

Such an attitude is in sharp contrast to the undisguised passionate persuasion of Marvell's *To His Coy Mistress,*

> ". . . while thy willing Soul transpires
> At every Pore with instant Fires,
> Now let us sport us while we may . . ."

Elizabeth Barrett Browning writes in her sonnets that love is a distinct and everlasting phenomenon,

"But love me for love's sake that evermore
Thou may'st love on, through love's eternity."

She contradicts Marvell's idea that love ends in the grave by stating,

"I love thee with the breath,
Smiles, tears, of all my life! - and, if God choose,
I shall but love thee better after death."

In *Echoes And Memories*, Shelley hints at a similar theme,

"And so thy thoughts, when thou art gone,
Love itself shall slumber on."

Shakespeare correctly foresaw that his writings would long outlive his own body. He refers to the longevity of poetry as a medium for expressions of love, far more effective than gravestones or other stone memorials, when he writes,

"Not marble, nor the gilded monuments
Of princes, shall outlive this powerful rhyme;
But you shall shine more bright in these contents
Than unswept stone, besmear'd with sluttish time."

Not all of the poems in this book celebrate the joys of love: some focus on the anguish of lost or unavailable love, some on jealousy, while some would perhaps better be described as poems of 'lust'. All the poems have been selected to achieve a balance, a cross section of true 'classics' of the genre. The resulting mélange consitutes a thorough representation of the enduring power of love over all humankind.

Stewart Ferris and Alastair Williams

There Is A Garden In Her Face

There is a garden in her face,
Where roses and white lilies grow;
A heavenly paradise is that place,
Wherein all pleasant fruits do grow;
There cherries grow that none may buy
Till cherry ripe themselves do cry.

Those cherries fairly do enclose
Of orient pearl a double row,
Which, when her lovely laughter shows,
They look like rosebuds fill'd with snow;
Yet them no peer nor prince may buy
Till cherry ripe themselves do cry.

Her eyes like angels watch them still,
Her brows like bended bows do stand,
Threatening with piercing frowns to kill
All that approach with eye or hand
These sacred cherries to come nigh,
Till cherry ripe themselves do cry.

Richard Allison

Inconstancy Reproved

I do confess thou'rt smooth and fair
And I might have gone near to love thee,
Had I not found the slightest prayer
That lips could move, had power to move thee;
But I can let thee now alone
As worthy to be loved by none.

I do confess thou'rt sweet; yet find
Thee such an unthrift of thy sweets,
Thy favours are but like the wind
That kisseth everything it meets:
And since thou canst with more than one,
Thou'rt worthy to be kissed by none.

The morning rose that untouched stands
Armed with her briers, how sweet she smells!
But plucked and strained through ruder hands,
Her sweets no longer with her dwells:
But scent and beauty both are gone,
And leaves fall from her, one by one.

Such fate ere long will thee betide
When thou hast handled been awhile,
With sere flowers to be thrown aside;
And I shall sigh, while some will smile,
To see thy love to every one
Hath brought thee to be loved by none.

Sir Robert Ayton

The Question Answered

What is it men in women do require?
The lineaments of gratified desire.
What is it women do in men require?
The lineaments of gratified desire.

William Blake

I Laid Me Down Upon A Bank

I laid me down upon a bank
Where Love lay sleeping
I heard among the rushes dank
Weeping, Weeping.

Then I went to the heath and the wild
To the thistles and thorns of the waste
And they told me how they were beguil'd
Driven out, and compell'd to be chaste.

William Blake

Love's Secret

Never seek to tell thy love,
Love that never told can be;
For the gentle wind doth move
Silently, invisibly.

I told my love, I told my love,
I told her all my heart,
Trembling, cold, in ghastly fears,
Ah! she did depart.

Soon after she was gone from me,
A traveller came by,
Silently, invisibly:
He took her with a sigh.

William Blake

The Garden Of Love

I went to the Garden of Love,
And saw what I never had seen:
A Chapel was built in the midst,
Where I used to play on the green.

And the gates of this Chapel were shut,
And "Thou shalt not" writ over the door;
So I turn'd to the Garden of Love
That so many sweet flowers bore;

And I saw it was filled with graves,
And tombstones where flowers should be;
And Priests in black gowns were walking their round
And binding with briars my joys and desires.

William Blake

To My Dear And Loving Husband

If ever two were one, then surely we;
If ever man were loved by wife, then thee;
If ever wife was happy in a man,
Compare with me, ye women, if you can.
I prize thy love more than whole mines of gold,
Or all the riches that the East doth hold.
My love is such that rivers cannot quench,
Nor aught but love from thee give recompense.
Thy love is such I can no way repay;
The heavens reward thee manifold, I pray.
Then while we live in love let's so persevere
That when we live no more we may live ever.

Anne Bradstreet

Sonnet XLIII, From The Portuguese

How do I love thee? Let me count the ways.
I love thee to the depth and breadth and height
My soul can reach, when feeling out of sight
For the ends of Being and ideal Grace.
I love thee to the level of every day's
Most quiet need, by sun and candlelight.
I love thee freely, as men strive for Right;
I love thee purely, as they turn from Praise.
I love thee with the passion put to use
In my old griefs, and with my childhood's faith.
I love thee with a love I seemed to lose
With my lost saints, - I love thee with the breath,
Smiles, tears, of all my life! - and, if God choose,
I shall but love thee better after death.

Elizabeth Barrett Browning

Sonnet

Yet, love, mere love, is beautiful indeed
And worthy of acceptation. Fire is bright,
Let temple burn, or flax; an equal light
Leaps in the flame from cedar-plank or weed.
And love is fire. And when I say at need
I love thee . . . mark! . . . I love thee - in thy sight
I stand transfigured, glorified aright,
With conscience of the new rays that proceed
Out of my face toward thine. There's nothing low
In love, when love the lowest: meanest creatures
Who love God, God accepts while loving so.
And what I feel, across the inferior features
Of what I am, doth flash itself, and show
How that great work of Love enhances Nature's.

Elizabeth Barrett Browning

Sonnet

If thou must love me, let it be for nought
Except for love's sake only. Do not say
"I love her for her smile . . . her look . . . her way
Of speaking gently . . . for a trick of thought
That falls in well with mine, and certes brought
A sense of pleasant ease on such a day" ‑
For these things in themselves, Belovèd, may
Be changed, or change for thee ‑ and love, so wrought
May be unwrought so. Neither love me for
Thine own dear pity's wiping my cheeks dry ‑
A creature might forget to weep, who bore
Thy comfort long and lose thy love thereby!
But love me for love's sake that evermore
Thou may'st love on, through love's eternity.

Elizabeth Barrett Browning

Sonnet

First time he kissed me, he but only kissed
The fingers of this hand wherewith I write;
And ever since, it grew more clean and white,
Slow to world-greetings, quick with its "Oh, list,"
When the angels speak. A ring of amethyst
I could not wear here plainer to my sight,
Than that first kiss. The second passed in height
The first, and sought the forehead, and half missed,
Half falling on the hair. O beyond meed!
That was the chrism of love, which love's own crown,
With sanctifying sweetness, did precede.
The third, upon my lips, was folded down
In perfect, purple state; since when, indeed,
I have been proud and said, "My love, my own."

Elizabeth Barrett Browning

Sonnet

Indeed this very love which is my boast,
And which, when rising up from breast to brow,
Doth crown me with a ruby large enow
To draw men's eyes and prove the inner cost.
This love even, all my worth, to the uttermost,
I should not love withal, unless that thou
Hadst·set me an example, shown me how,
When first thine earnest eyes with mine were crossed
And love called love. And thus, I cannot speak
Of love even, as a good thing of my own.
Thy soul hath snatched up mine all faint and weak,
And placed it by thee on a golden throne-
And that I love (O soul, we must be meek!)
Is by thee only, whom I love alone.

Elizabeth Barrett Browning

Sonnet

When our two souls stand up erect and strong,
Face to face, silent, drawing nigh and nigher,
Until the lengthening wings break into fire
At either curvèd point - what bitter wrong
Can the earth do to us, that we should not long
Be here contented? Think. In mounting higher
The angels would press on us and aspire
To drop some golden orb of perfect song
Into our deep, dear silence. Let us stay
Rather on earth, Belovèd - where the unfit
Contrarious moods of men recoil away
And isolate pure spirits, and permit
A place to stand and love in for a day,
With darkness and the death-hour rounding it.

Elizabeth Barrett Browning

Sonnet

I think of thee! my thoughts do twine and bud
About thee, as wild vines, about a tree,
Put out broad leaves, and soon there's nought to see
Except the straggling green which hides the wood.
Yet, O my palm-tree, be it understood
I will not have my thoughts instead of thee
Who art dearer, better! Rather, instantly
Renew thy presence, as a strong tree should,
Rustle thy boughs and set thy trunk all bare
And let these bands of greenery which insphere thee,
Drop heavily down . . . burst, shattered, everywhere!
Because, in this deep joy to see and hear thee,
And breathe within thy shadow a new air,
I do not think of thee - I am too near thee.

Elizabeth Barrett Browning

Sonnet

Belovèd, thou hast brought me many flowers
Plucked in the garden, all the summer through
And winter, and it seemed as if they grew
In this close room, nor missed the sun and showers.
So, in the like name of that love of ours,
Take back these thoughts which here unfolded too,
And which on warm and cold days I withdrew
From my heart's ground. Indeed, those beds and bowers
Be overgrown with bitter weeds and rue,
And wait thy weeding; yet here's eglantine,
Here's ivy! take them, as I used to do
Thy flowers, and keep them where they shall not pine.
Instruct thine eyes to keep their colours true,
And tell thy soul, their roots are left in mine.

Elizabeth Barrett Browning

Sonnet

Belovèd, my Belovèd, when I think
That thou wast in the world a year ago,
What time I sat alone here in the snow
And saw no footprint, heard the silence sink
No moment at thy voice, but, link by link,
Went counting all my chains as if that so
They never could fall off at any blow
Struck by thy possible hand why, thus I drink
Of life's great cup of wonder! Wonderful
Never to feel thee thrill the day or night
With personal act or speech - nor even cull
Some prescience of thee with the blossoms white
Thou sawest growing! Atheists are as dull,
Who cannot guess God's presence out of sight.

Elizabeth Barrett Browning

Sonnet

And wilt thou have me fashion into speech
The love I bear thee, finding words enough,
And hold the torch out, while the winds are rough
Between our faces, to cast light on each?
I drop it at thy feet. I cannot teach
My hand to hold my spirit so far off
From myself . . . me . . . that I should bring thee proof
In words, of love hid in me out of reach.
Nay, let the silence of my womanhood
Commend my woman-love to thy belief,
Seeing that I stand unwon, however wooed,
And rend the garment of my life, in brief,
By a most dauntless, voiceless fortitude,
Lest one touch of this heart convey its grief.

Elizabeth Barrett Browning

Sonnet

If I leave all for thee, wilt thou exchange
And be all to me? Shall I never miss
Home-talk and blessing, and the common kiss
That comes to each in turn, nor count it strange,
When I look up, to drop on a new range
Of walls and floors, another home than this?
Nay, wilt thou fill that place by me which is
Filled by dead eyes too tender to know change?
That's hardest. If to conquer love, has tried,
To conquer grief, tries more, as all things prove
For grief indeed is love and grief beside.
Alas, I have grieved so I am hard to love.
Yet love me - wilt thou? Open thine heart wide,
And fill within, the wet wings of thy dove.

Elizabeth Barrett Browning

You

God be thanked, the meanest of his creatures
Boasts two soul-sides, one to face the world with,
One to show a woman when he loves her.

This I say of me, but think of you, love!
This to you - yourself, my moon of poets!
Ah, but that's the world's side, there's the wonder
Thus they see you, praise you, think they know you!
There, in turn I stand with them and praise you -
Out of my own self, I dare to phrase it.

But the best is when I glide from out them,
Cross a step or two of dubious twilight,
Come out on the other side, the novel
Silent silver lights and darks undreamed of
Where I hush and bless myself with silence.

Oh, their Raphael of the dear Madonnas,
Oh, their Dante of the dread Inferno,
Wrote one song - and in my brain I sing it,
Drew one angel - borne, see, on my bosom!

Robert Browning

Life In A Love

Escape me?
Never -
Beloved!
While I am I, and you are you,
So long as the world contains us both,
Me the loving and you the loth,
While the one eludes, must the other pursue.
My life is a fault at last, I fear:
It seems too much like a fate, indeed!
Though I do my best I shall scarce succeed.
But what if I fail of my purpose here?
It is but to keep the nerves at strain,
To dry one's eyes and laugh at a fall
And, baffled, get up to begin again -
So the chase takes up one's life, that's all.
While, look but once from your farthest bound
At me so deep in the dust and dark,
No sooner the old hope drops to ground
Than a new one, straight to the self-same mark
I shape me -
Ever
Removed!

Robert Browning

Never The Time And The Place

Never the time and the place
And the loved one all together!
This path - how soft to pace!
This May - what magic weather!
Where is the loved one's face?
In a dream that loved one's face meets mine,
But the house is narrow, the place is bleak
Where, outside, rain and wind combine
With a furtive ear, if I strive to speak,
With hostile eye at my flushing cheek,
With a malice that marks each word, each sign!
O enemy sly and serpentine
Uncoil thee from the waking man!
Do I hold the past
Thus firm and fast
Yet doubt if the future hold I can
This path so soft to pace shall lead,
Thro' the magic of May to herself indeed!
Or narrow if needs the house must be,
Outside are the storms and strangers: we -
Oh, close, safe, warm sleep I and she,
- I and she!

Robert Browning

A Red Red Rose

O my Luve's like a red, red rose,
That's newly sprung in June;
O my Luve's like the melodie
That's sweetly play'd in tune.

As fair art thou, my bonie lass,
So deep in luve am I;
And I will love thee still, my Dear,
Till a' the seas gang dry.

Till a' the seas gang dry, my Dear,
And the rocks melt wi' the sun:
I will love thee still, my Dear,
While the sands o' life shall run.

And fare thee weel, my only Luve!
And fare thee weel, a while!
And I will come again, my Luve,
Tho' it were ten thousand mile!

Robert Burns

I Love My Jean

Of a'the airts the wind can blaw,
I dearly like the west,
For there the bonnie Lassie lives,
The Lassie I lo'e best.
There wild woods grow, and rivers row,
And mony a hill's between;
But day and night my fancy's flight
Is ever wi' my Jean.

I see her in the dewy flowers,
I see her sweet and fair;
I hear her in the tunefu' birds
I hear her charm the air;
There's not a bonnie flower that springs
By fountain, shaw, or green;
There's not a bonnie bird that sings
But minds me o' my Jean.

Robert Burns

One Fond Kiss And Then We Sever

One fond kiss, and then we sever!
One farewell, and then forever!
Deep in heart-wrung tears I'll pledge thee
Warring sighs and groans I'll wage thee.

Who shall say that Fortune grieves him,
While the star of Hope she leaves him?
Me, no cheerful twinkle lights me;
Dark despair around benights me.

I'll ne'er blame my partial fancy,
Nothing could resist my Nancy:
But to see her was to love her;
Love but her, and love forever.

Had we never loved so kindly,
Had we never loved so blindly,
Never met or never parted,
We had ne'er been broken-hearted.

Fare thee well, thou first and fairest!
Fare thee well, thou best and dearest!
Thine be every joy and treasure,
Peace, enjoyment, love, and pleasure!

One fond kiss, and then we sever!
One farewell, alas, for ever!
Deep in heart-wrung tears I'll pledge thee,
Warring sighs and groans I'll wage thee.

Robert Burns

Had I A Cave

Had I a cave on some wild, distant shore,
Where the winds howl to the waves' dashing roar,
  There would I weep my woes,
  There seek my lost repose,
  Till grief my eyes should close,
  Ne'er to wake more!

Falsest of womankind' canst thou declare
All thy fond-plighted vows - fleeting as air!
  To thy new lover hie,
  Laugh o'er thy perjury;
  Then in thy bosom try
  What peace is there!

Robert Burns

She Walks In Beauty

She walks in Beauty, like the night
Of cloudless climes and starry skies;
And all that's best of dark and bright
Meet in her aspect and her eyes:
Thus mellowed to that tender light
Which Heaven to gaudy day denies.

One shade the more, one ray the less,
Had half impaired the nameless grace
Which waves in every raven tress,
Or softly lightens o'er her face;
Where thoughts serenely sweet express
How pure, how dear their dwelling place.

And on that cheek, and o'er that brow,
So soft, so calm, yet eloquent,
The smiles that win, the tints that glow,
But tell of days in goodness spent,
A mind at peace with all below,
A heart whose love is innocent!

Lord Byron

Stanzas For Music

There be none of Beauty's daughters
With a magic like thee;
And like music on the waters
Is thy sweet voice to me:
When, as if its sound were causing
The charmèd Ocean's pausing,
The waves lie still and gleaming,
And the lull'd winds seem dreaming.

And the Midnight Moon is weaving
Her bright chain o'er the deep;
Whose breast is gently heaving,
As an infant's asleep:
So the spirit bows before thee,
To listen and adore thee;
With a full but soft emotion,
Like the swell of Summer's ocean.

Lord Byron

On Parting

The kiss, dear maid! thy lip has left
Shall never part from mine,
Till happier hours restore the gift
Untainted back to thine.

Thy parting glance, which fondly beams,
An equal love may see:
The tear that from thine eyelid streams
Can weep no change in me.

I ask no pledge to make me blest
In gazing when alone;
Nor one memorial for a breast
Whose thoughts are all thine own.

Nor need I write - to tell the tale
My pen were doubly weak:
Oh! what can idle words avail,
Unless the heart could speak?

By day or night, in weal or woe,
That heart, no longer free,
Must bear the love it cannot show,
And silent ache for thee.

Lord Byron

To Ellen

Oh! might I kiss those eyes of fire,
A million scarce would quench desire:
Still would I steep my lips in bliss,
And dwell an age on every kiss;
Nor then my soul should sated be,
Still would I kiss and cling to thee:
Nought should my kiss from thine dissever;
Still would we kiss, and kiss forever,
E'en though the numbers did exceed
The yellow harvest's countless seed.
To part would be a vain endeavor:
Could I desist? Ah, never-never!

Lord Byron

Maid Of Athens

Maid of Athens, ere we part,
Give, oh give me back my heart!
Or, since that has left my breast,
Keep it now, and take the rest
Hear my vow before I go,
Zoë mou, sas agapo.

By those tresses unconfin'd,
Woo'd by each Aegean wind;
By those lids whose jetty fringe
Kiss thy soft cheeks' blooming tinge;
By those wild eyes like the roe,
Zoë mou, sas agapo.

By that lip I long to taste,
By that zone-encircl'd waist,
By all the token-flowers that tell
What words can never speak so well;
By love's alternate joy and woe,
Zoë mou, sas agapo.

Maid of Athens! I am gone:
Think of me, sweet! when alone.
Though I fly to Istambol,
Athens holds my heart and soul:
Can I cease to love thee? No!
Zoë mou, sas agapo.

Lord Byron

Oh! Snatched Away In Beauty's Bloom

Oh! snatched away in Beauty's bloom,
On thee shall press no ponderous tomb;
But on thy turf shall roses rear
Their leaves, the earliest of the year;
And the wild cypress wave in tender gloom:

And oft by yon blue gushing stream
Shall Sorrow lean her drooping head,
And feed deep thought with many a dream,
and lingering pause and lightly tread;
Fond wretch! as if her step disturbed the dead!

Away! we know that tears are vain,
That Death nor heeds nor hears distress;
Will this unteach us to complain?
Or make one mourner weep the less?
And thou - who tell'st me to forget
Thy looks are wan, thine eyes are wet.

Lord Byron

When We Two Parted

When we two parted
In silence and tears,
Half broken-hearted,
To sever for years,
Pale grew thy cheek and cold,
Colder thy kiss;
Truly that hour foretold
Sorrow to this.

The dew of the morning
Sunk chill on my brow -
It felt like the warning
Of what I feel now.
Thy vows are all broken,
And light is thy fame;
I hear thy name spoken,
And share in its shame.

They name thee before me,
A knell to mine ear;
A shudder comes o'er me -
Why wert thou so dear?
They know not I knew thee,
Who knew thee too well:
Long, long shall I rue thee,
Too deeply to tell.

In secret we met -
In silence I grieve,
That thy heart could forget,
Thy spirit deceive.
If I should meet thee,
After long years,
How should I greet thee!
With silence and tears.

Lord Byron

Freedom And Love

How delicious is the winning
Of a kiss at Love's beginning,
When two mutual hearts are sighing
For the knot there's no untying!

Yet remember, 'midst our wooing
Love has bliss, but Love has ruing;
Other smiles may make you fickle,
Tears for other charms may trickle.

Love he comes, and Love he tarries,
Just as fate or fancy carries;
Longest stays, when sorest chidden;
Laughs and flies, when press'd and bidden.

Bind the sea to slumber stilly,
Bind its odour to the lily,
Bind the aspen ne'er to quiver,
Then bind Love to last forever.

Love's a fire that needs renewal
Of fresh beauty for its fuel:
Love's wing moults when caged and captured,
Only free, he soars enraptured.

Can you keep the bee from ranging
Or the ringdove's neck from changing?
No! nor fetter'd Love from dying
In the knot there's no untying.

Thomas Campbell

My Lady's Eyes

Mistress, since you so much desire
To know the place of Cupid's fire
In your fair shrine that flame doth rest,
Yet never harboured in your breast.

It bides not in your lips so sweet,
Nor where the rose and lilies meet;
But a little higher, a little higher,
There, there, O there lies Cupid's fire.

Even in those starry piercing eyes,
There Cupid's sacred fire lies;
Those eyes I strive not to enjoy,
For they have power to destroy:

Nor woo for a smile or kiss,
So meanly triumphs not my bliss;
But a little higher, a little higher
I climb to crown my chaste desire.

Thomas Campion

The Plea

Kind in unkindness, when will you relent
And cease with faint love true love to torment?
Still entertained, excluded still I stand,
Her glove still hold, but cannot touch her hand.

In her fair hand my hopes and comforts rest:
O might my fortunes with that hand be blest!
No envious breaths then my deserts could shake
For they are good whom such true love doth make.

O let not beauty so forget her birth
That it should fruitless home return to earth!
Love is the fruit of beauty, then love one -
Not your sweet self, for such self-love is none.

Love one that only lives in loving you,
Whose wronged deserts would you with pity view.
This strange distaste which your affection sways
Would relish love, and you find better days.

Thus till my happy sight your beauty views,
Whose sweet remembrance still my hope renews,
Let these poor lines solicit love for me
And place my joys where my desires would be.

Thomas Campion

Come, O Come

Come, O come, my life's delight,
Let me not in languor pine!
Love loves no delay; thy sight,
The more enjoyed, the more divine:
O come, and take from me
The pain of being deprived of thee!

Thou all sweetness dost enclose,
Like a little world of bliss.
Beauty guards thy looks: the rose
In them pure and eternal is.
Come, then, and make thy flight
As swift to me, as heavenly light.

Thomas Campion

The Compliment

I do not love thee for that fair
Rich fan of thy most curious hair;
Though the wires thereof be drawn
Finer than the threads of lawn,
And are softer than the leaves
On which the subtle spider weaves.

I do not love thee for those flowers
Growing on thy cheeks - love's bowers;
Though such cunning them hath spread,
None can paint them white and red:
Love's golden arrows thence are shot
Yet for them I love thee not.

I do not love thee for those soft
Red coral lips I've kissed so oft;
Nor teeth of pearl, the double guard
To speech whence music still is heard,
Though from those lips a kiss being taken
Might tyrants melt, and death awaken.

I do not love thee, O my fairest,
For that richest, for that rarest
Silver pillar, which stands under
Thy sound head, that globe of wonder;
Though that neck be whiter far
Than towers of polished ivory are.

Thomas Carew

Red And White Roses

Read in these Roses the sad story
Of my hard fate, and your owne glory.
In the White you may discover
The paleness of a fainting lover;
In the Red the flames still feeding
On my heart, with fresh wounds bleeding.
The White will tell you how I languish,
And the Red express my anguish;
The White my innocence displaying,
The Red my martyrdom betraying.
The frowns that on your brow resided,
Have those Roses thus divided.
Oh! let your smiles but clear the weather,
And then they both shall grow together.

Thomas Carew

Song: To My Inconstant Mistress

When thou, poor excommunicate
From all the joys of love, shalt see
The full reward and glorious fate
Which my strong faith shall purchase me,
Then curse thine own inconstancy.

A fairer hand than thine shall cure
That heart, which thy false oaths did wound;
And to my soul a soul more pure
Than thine shall by Love's hand be bound
And both with equal glory crown'd.

Then shalt thou weep, entreat, complain
To Love, as I did once to thee;
When all thy tears shall be as vain
As mine were then, for thou shalt be
Damn'd for thy false apostasy.

Thomas Carew

Song: Mediocrity In Love Rejected

Give me more love or more disdain;
The torrid or the frozen zone
Bring equal ease unto my pain,
The temperate affords me none:
Either extreme of love or hate,
Is sweeter than a calm estate.

Give me a storm; if it be love,
Like Danaë in that golden shower,
I swim in pleasure; if it prove
Disdain, that torrent will devour
My vulture hopes; and he's possess'd
Of heaven, that's but from hell released.
Then crown my joys or cure my pain:
Give me more love or more disdain.

Thomas Carew

Lips And Eyes

In Celia's face a question did arise:
Which were more beautiful, her lips or eyes.
'We,' said the eyes, 'send forth those pointed darts
Which pierce the hardest adamantine hearts.'
'From us,' replied the lips, 'proceed those blisses
Which lovers reap by kind words and sweet kisses.'
Then wept the eyes, and from their springs did pour
Of liquid oriental pearl a shower,
Whereat the lips, moved with delight and pleasure,
Through a sweet smile unlocked their pearly treasure,
And bade Love judge whether did add more grace
Weeping or smiling pearls to Celia's face.

Thomas Carew

No Platonic Love

Tell me no more of minds embracing minds,
And hearts exchang'd for hearts;
That spirits spirits meet, as winds do winds,
And mix their subt'lest parts;
That two unbodied essences may kiss,
And then like angels, twist and feel one bliss.

I was that silly thing that once was wrought
To practise this thin love;
I climb'd from sex to soul, from soul to thought;
But thinking there to move,
Headlong I roll'd from thought to soul, and then
From soul I lighted at the sex agen.

As some strict down-look'd men pretend to fast
Who yet in closets eat;
So lovers who profess they spirits taste,
Feed yet on grosser meat;
I know they boast they souls to souls convey,
Howe'er they meet, the body is the way.

Come, I will undeceive thee, they that tread
Those vain aerial ways,
Are like young heirs and alchymists misled
To waste their wealth and days,
For searching thus to be for ever rich,
They only find a med'cine for the itch.

William Cartwright

To Chloe, Who For His Sake Wished Herself Younger

There are two births; the one when light
First strikes the new awaken'd sense;
The other when two souls unite,
And we must count our life from thence:
When you loved me and I loved you
The both of us were born anew.

Love then to us new souls did give
And in those souls did plant new powers;
Since when another life we live,
The breath we breathe is his, not ours:
Love makes those young whom age doth chill,
And whom he finds young keeps young still.

William Cartwright

From The Knight's Tale

And so bifel, by aventure or cas,
That thurgh a wyndow, thikke of many a barre
Of iren greet and square as any sparre,
He cast his eye upon Emelya,
And therwithal he bleynte and cride, "A!"
As though he stongen were unto the herte.
And with that cry Arcite anon up sterte
And seyde, "Cosyn myn, what eyleth thee,
That art so pale and deedly on to see?
Why cridestow? Who hath thee doon offence?
For Goddes love, taak al in pacience
Oure prisoun, for it may noon other be.
Fortune hath yeven us this adversitee.
Som wikke aspect or disposicioun
Of Saturne, by som constellacioun,
Hath yeven us this, although we had it sworn;
So stood the hevene whan that we were born.
We moste endure it; this is the short and playn."
This Palamon answerde and sayde agayn,
"Cosyn, for sothe, of this opinioun
Thou hast a veyn ymaginacioun.
This prison caused me nat for to crye,
But I was hurt right now thurghout myn ye
Into myn herte, that wol my bane be.
The fairnesse of that lady that I see
Yond in the gardyn romen to and fro
Is cause of al my criyng and my wo.
I noot wher she be womman or goddesse,
But Venus is it soothly, as I gesse."

And therwithal on knees doun he fil,
And seyde, "Venus, if it be thy wil
Yow in this gardyn thus to transfigure
Bifore me, sorweful, wrecched creature,
Out of this prisoun help that we may scapen.
And if so be my destynee be shapen
By eterne word to dyen in prisoun,
Of oure lynage have som compassioun,
That is so lowe ybroght by tirannye."
And with that word Arcite gan espye
Wher as this lady romed to and fro,
And with that sighte hir beautee hurte hym so,
That, if that Palamon was wounded sore,
Arcite is hurt as muche as he, or moore.
And with a sigh he seyde pitously,
"The fresshe beautee sleeth me sodeynly
Of hire that rometh in the yonder place;
And but I have hir mercy and hir grace,
That I may seen hire atte leeste weye,
I nam but deed; ther nis namoore to seye."

Geoffrey Chaucer

From The Miller's Tale

"Allas," quod Absolon, "and weylawey,
That trewe love was evere so yvel biset!
Thanne kysse me, syn it may be no bet,
For Jhesus love, and for the love of me."
"Wiltow thanne go thy wey therwith?" quod she.
"Ye, certes, lemman," quod this Absolon.
"Thanne make thee redy," quod she, "I come anon."
And unto Nicholas she seyde stille,
"Now hust, and thou shalt laughen al thy fille."
This Absolon doun sette hym on his knees
And seyde, "I am a lord at alle degrees;
For after this I hope ther cometh moore.
Lemman, thy grace, and sweete bryd, thyn oore!"
The wyndow she undoth, and that in haste.
"Have do," quod she, "com of, and speed the faste,
Lest that oure neighebores thee espie."
This Absolon gan wype his mouth ful drie.
Derk was the nyght as pich, or as cole,
And at the wyndow out she putte hir hole,
And Absolon, hym fil no bet ne wers,
But with his mouth he kiste hir naked ers
Ful savourly, er he were war of this.
Abak he stirte, and thoughte it was amys,
For wel he wiste a womman hath no berd.

Geoffrey Chaucer

The Faithful And The True

Love lives beyond
The tomb, the earth, which fades like dew
I love the fond,
The faithfull, and the true.

Love lives in sleep,
The happiness of healthy dreams:
Eve's dews may weep,
But love delightful seems.

'Tis seen in flowers,
And in the morning's pearly dew;
On earth's green hours
And in the heaven's eternal blue.

'Tis heard in spring
When light and sunbeams, warm and kind,
On angel's wing
Bring love and music to the mind.

And where is voice,
So young, so beautiful, and sweet
As nature's choice,
Where spring and lovers meet.

Love lives beyond
The tomb, the earth, the flowers, and dew.
I love the fond,
The faithful, young, and true.

John Clare

First Love

I ne'er was struck before that hour
With love so sudden and so sweet;
Her face it bloomed like a sweet flower
And stole my heart away complete.
My face turned pale as deadly pale,
My legs refused to walk away,
And when she looked what could I ail?
My life and all seemed turned to clay.

And then my blood rushed to my face
And took my eyesight quite away;
The trees and bushes round the place
Seemed midnight at noonday.
I could not see a single thing,
Words from my eyes did start;
They spoke as chords do from the string
And blood burnt round my heart.

Are flowers the winter's choice?
Is love's bed always snow?
She seemed to hear my silent voice,
Not love's appeals to know.
I never saw so sweet a face
As that I stood before;
My heart has left its dwelling place
And can return no more.

John Clare

Love's Pains

This love, I canna' bear it,
It cheats me night and day;
This love, I canna' wear it
It takes my peace away.

This love, wa' once a flower;
But now it is a thorn -
The joy o' evening hour,
Turn'd to a pain e're morn.

This love, it wa' a bud,
And a secret known to me;
Like a flower within a wood;
Like a nest within a tree.

This love, wrong understood,
Oft' turned my joy to pain;
I tried to throw away the bud,
But the blossom would remain.

John Clare

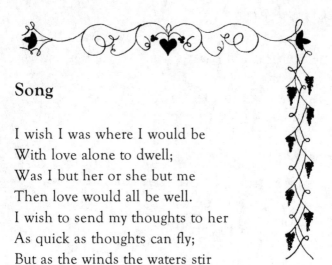

Song

I wish I was where I would be
With love alone to dwell;
Was I but her or she but me
Then love would all be well.
I wish to send my thoughts to her
As quick as thoughts can fly;
But as the winds the waters stir
The mirrors change and flye.

John Clare

I Hid My Love

I hid my love when young while I
Could'nt bear the buzzing of a flye;
I hid my love to my despite
Till I could not bear to look at light.
I dare not gaze upon her face
But left her memory in each place,
Where ere I saw a wildflower lye
I kissed and bade my love good bye.

I met her in the greenest dells
Where dewdrops pearl the wood bluebells;
The lost breeze kissed her bright blue eye
The bee kissed and went singing by.
A sunbeam found a passage there,
A gold chain round her neck so fair;
As secret as the wild bee's song,
She lay there all the summer long.

I hid my love in field and town
Till e'en the breeze would knock me down;
The bees seemed singing ballads o'er
The fly's buzz turned a lion's roar.
And even silence found a tongue
To haunt me all the summer long;
The riddle nature could not prove
Was nothing else but secret love.

John Clare

Love's Memories

Love's memories haunt my footsteps still
    Like ceaseless flowings of the river.
Its mystic depths say what can fill?
    Sad disappointment waits forever.

John Clare

To Mary

I sleep with thee, and wake with thee,
And yet thou art not there;
I fill my arms with thoughts of thee,
And press the common air.
Thy eyes are gazing upon mine,
When thou art out of sight;
My lips are always touching thine,
At morning, noon, and night.

I think and speak of other things
To keep my mind at rest:
But still to thee my memory clings
Like love in woman's breast.
I hide it from the world's wide eye
And think and speak contrary;
But soft the wind comes from the sky,
And whispers tales of Mary.

The night wind whispers in my ear,
The moon shines in my face;
A burden still of chilling fear
I find in every place.
The breeze is whispering in the bush,
And the dews fall from the tree,
All, sighing on, and will not hush
Some pleasant tales of thee.

John Clare

The Exchange

We pledged our hearts, my love and I,
I in my arms the maiden clasping;
I could not tell the reason why,
But, O, I trembled like an aspen.

Her father's love she bade me gain;
I went, and shook like any reed!
I strove to act the man - in vain!
We had exchanged our hearts indeed.

Samuel Taylor Coleridge

The Happy Husband

Oft, oft, methinks, the while with thee
I breathe, as from the heart, thy dear
And dedicated name, I hear
A promise and a mystery,
A pledge of more than passing life,
Yea, in that very name of Wife!

A pulse of love that ne'er can sleep!
A feeling that upbraids the heart
With happiness beyond desert,
That gladness half requests to weep!
Nor bless I not the keener sense
And unalarming turbulence.

Of transient joys, that ask no sting
From jealous fears, or coy denying;
But born beneath Love's brooding wing
And into tenderness soon dying,
Wheel out their giddy moment, then
Resign the soul to love again;

A more precipitated vein
Of notes that eddy in the flow
Of smoothest song, they come, they go,
And leave their sweeter understrain
Its own sweet self - a love of Thee
That seems, yet cannot greater be!

Samuel Taylor Coleridge

Song

See, see, she wakes, Sabina wakes!
And now the sun begins to rise;
Less glorious is the morn that breaks
From his bright beams than her fair eyes.

With light united, day they give,
But different fates ere night fulfill.
How many by his warmth will live!
How many will her coldness kill!

William Congreve

Sonnet

My lady's presence makes the roses red
Because to see her lips they blush for shame;
The lily's leaves, for envy, pale became,
For her white hands in them this envy bred.
The marigold the leaves abroad doth spread,
Because the sun's and her power is the same
The violet of purple colour came,
Dyed in the blood she made my heart to shed.
In brief, all flowers from her their virtue take;
From her sweet breath their sweet smells do proceed;
The living heat which her eyebeams do make
Warmeth the ground, and quickeneth the seed.
The rain, wherewith she watereth the flowers,
Falls from mine eyes, which she dissolves in showers.

Henry Constable

The Marriage Ring

The ring, so worn as you behold,
So thin, so pale, is yet of gold:
The passion such it was to prove -
Worn with life's care, love yet was love.

George Crabbe

He Touched Me

He touched me, so I live to know
That such a day, permitted so,
I groped upon his breast.
It was a boundless place to me,
And silenced, as the awful sea
Puts minor streams to rest.

And now, I'm different from before,
As if I breathed superior air,
Or brushed a Royal Gown;
My feet, too, that had wandered so,
My Gypsy Face transfigured now
To tenderer Renown.

Into this Port, if I might come,
Rebecca, to Jerusalem,
Would not so ravished turn -
Nor Persian, baffled at her shrine
Lift such a crucifixal sign
To her imperial sun.

Emily Dickinson

Longing

I envy Seas whereon he rides,
I envy Spokes of Wheels
Of Chariots that him convey,
I envy crooked Hills

That gaze upon his journey;
How easy all can see
What is forbidden utterly
As Heaven, unto me!

I envy Nests of Sparrows
That dot his distant Eaves,
The wealthy Fly upon his Pane,
The happy, happy Leaves

That just abroad his Window
Have Summer's leave to be,
The Ear Rings of Pizarro
Could not obtain for me.

I envy Light that wakes him,
And Bells - that boldly ring
To tell him it is Noon abroad-
Myself be Noon to him,

Yet interdict my Blossom
And abrogate my Bee,
Lest Noon in everlasting Night
Drop Gabriel and me.

Emily Dickinson

Heart, We Will Forget Him

Heart, we will forget him!
You and I, tonight!
You may forget the warmth he gave,
I will forget the light.

When you have done, pray tell me,
That I may straight begin!
Haste! lest while you're lagging,
I may remember him!

Emily Dickinson

The Flea

Marke but this flea, and marke in this,
How little that which thou deny'st me is;
Me it suck'd first, and now sucks thee,
And in this flea, our two bloods mingled be;
Thou know'st that this cannot be said
A sin, or shame, or loss of maidenhead,
Yet this enjoyes before it woo,
And pampered swells with one blood made of two,
And this, alas, is more than we would do.

Oh stay, three lives in one flea spare,
Where we almost, yea more than maryed are:
This flea is you and I, and this
Our marriage bed, and marriage temple is;
Though parents grudge, and you, we're met,
And cloystered in these living walls of jet.
Though use make thee apt to kill me,
Let not to this, selfe murder added be,
And sacrilege, three sinnes in killing three.

Cruel and sodaine, hast thou since
Purpled thy naile, in blood of innocence?
Wherein could this flea guilty be,
Except in that drop which it sucked from thee?
Yet thou triumph'st, and say'st that thou
Find'st not thy selfe, nor me the weaker now;
'Tis true, then learn how false, fears be;
Just so much honor, when thou yeeld'st to me,
Will waste, as this flea's death took life from thee.

John Donne

A Lecture Upon The Shadow

Stand still, and I will read to thee
A Lecture, Love, in love's philosophy.
 These three hours that we have spent,
 Walking here, Two shadowes went
Along with us, which we ourselves produced;
But, now the Sunne is just above our head,
 We do those shadowes tread;
 And to brave clearnesse all things are reduced.
So whilst our infant loves did grow,
Disguises did, and shadows, flow,
From us, and our care; but, now 'tis not so.

That love hath not attained the high'st degree
Which is still diligent lest others see.

Except our loves at this noone stay,
We shall new shadows make the other way.
 As the first were made to blinde
 Others; these which come behinde
Will work upon ourselves, and blind our eyes.
If our loves faint, and westwardly decline;
 To me thou, falsely, thine,
 And I to thee mine actions shall disguise.
The morning shadowes wear away,
But these grow longer all the day,
But oh, love's day is short, if love decay.

Love is a growing, or full constant light;
And his first minute, after noon, is night.

John Donne

Breake Of Day

Stay, O sweet, and do not rise!
The light, that shines, comes from thine eyes.
The day breaks not: it is my heart,
Because that you and I must part.
Stay, or else my joys will die,
And perish in their infancy.

'Tis true, 'tis day, what though it be?
O wilt thou therefore rise from me?
Why should we rise, because 'tis light?
Did we lie downe, because t'was night?
Love, which in spite of darknesse brought us hither,
Should in despite of light keep us together.

Light hath no tongue, but is all eye.
If it could speak as well as spie,
This were the worst that it could say,
That, being well, I faine would stay,
And that I lov'd my heart and honour so
That I would not from her, that had them, go.

Must business thee from hence remove?
O, that's the worst disease of love,
The poore, the foule, the false, love can,
Admit, but not the busied man.
He, which hath businesse, and makes love, doth do
Such wrong, as when a maryed man doth woo.

John Donne

The Apparition

When by thy scorn, O murdresse, I am dead,
And that thou thinkst thee free
From all solicitation from me,
Then shall my ghost come to thy bed,
And thee, fain'd vestal, in worse arms shall see;
Then thy sicke taper will begin to winke,
And he, whose thou art then, being tyr'd before,
Will, if thou stire, or pinch to wake him, thinke
Thou call'st for more,
And in false sleep will from thee shrink,
And then poore Aspen wretch, neglected thou
Bath'd in a cold quicksilver sweat wilt lye
A veryer ghost than I;
What I will say, I will not tell thee now,
Lest that preserve thee' and since my love is spent,
I had rather thou shouldst painfully repent,
Than by my threatnings rest still innocent.

John Donne

April Love

We have walked in Love's land a little way
We have learnt his lesson a little while,
And shall we not part at the end of day,
With a sigh, a smile?

A little while in the shine of the sun,
We were twined together, joined lips forgot
How the shadows fall when the day is done,
And when Love is not.

We have made no vows - there will none be broke,
Our love was free as the wind on the hill,
There was no word said we need wish unspoke,
We have wrought no ill.

So shall we not part at the end of day,
Who have loved and lingered a little while,
Join lips for the last time, go our way,
With a sigh, a smile.

Ernest Dowson

Ah, How Sweet

Ah, how sweet it is to love,
Ah, how gay is young desire!
And what pleasing pains we prove
When we first approach Love's fire!
Pains of Love are sweeter far
Than all other pleasures are.

Sighs which are from Lovers blown
Do but gently heave the Heart:
Ev'n the tears they shed alone
Cure, like trickling Balm, their smart.
Lovers, when they lose their breath,
Bleed away in easie death.

Love and Time with reverence use,
Treat 'em like a parting friend:
Nor the golden gifts refuse
Which in youth sincere they send:
For each year their price is more,
And they less simple than before.

Love, like Spring-tides full and high,
Swells in every youthful vein:
But each Tide does less supply,
Till they quite shrink in again.
If a flow in Age appear,
'Tis but rain, and runs not clear.

John Dryden

The Suffering Heart

No, no, poor suff'ring Heart, no change endeavour;
Choose to sustain the smart, rather than leave her.
My ravish'd Eyes behold such charms about her,
I can dye with her, but not live without her.
One tender Sigh of hers, to see me languish,
Will more than pay the price of my past Anguish.
Beware, O cruel fair, how you smile on me,
'Twas a kind Look of yours that has undone me.

Love has in store for me one happy Minute,
And she will end my pain who did begin it;
Then, no day void of bliss or pleasure leaving,
Ages shall slide away without perceiving:
Cupid shall guard the Door, the more to please us,
And keep out Time and Death, when they would
        seize us:
Time and Death shall depart, and say, in flying,
Love has found out a way to live by dying.

John Drydren

To A Lady
How Long He Would Love Her

It is not, Celia, in our power
To say how long our love will last;
It may be we within this hour
May lose those joys we now do taste:
The blessed, that immortal be,
From change in love are only free.

Then since we mortal lovers are,
Ask not how long our love will last;
But while it does, let us take care
Each minute be with pleasure passed:
Were it not madness to deny
To live because we're sure to die?

George Etherege

I Love My Love In The Morning

I love my love in the morning,
For she like morn is fair ·
Her blushing cheek, its crimson streak,
It clouds her golden hair.
Her glance, its beam, so soft and kind;
Her tears, its dewy showers;
And her voice, the tender whispering wind
That stirs the early bowers.

I love my love in the morning,
I love my love at noon,
For she is bright as the lord of light,
Yet mild as autumn's moon:
Her beauty is my bosom's sun
Her faith my fostering shade,
And I will love my darling one,
Till even the sun shall fade.

I love my love in the morning,
I love my love at even;
Her smile's soft play is like the ray
That lights the western heaven:
I loved her when the sun was high,
I loved her when he rose;
But best of all when evening's sigh
Was murmuring at its close.

Gerald Griffin

To The Virgins,
To Make Much Of Time

Gather ye Rose-buds while ye may,
Old Time is still a-flying:
And this same flower that smiles today
Tomorrow will be dying.

The glorious Lamp of Heaven, the Sun,
The higher he's a-getting,
The sooner will his Race be run
And nearer he's to Setting.

That Age is best which is the first,
When Youth and Blood are warmer;
But being spent, the worse, and worst
Times still succeed the former.

Then be not coy, but use your time,
And while ye may, go marry:
For having lost but once your prime,
You may for ever tarry.

Robert Herrick

To Anthea, who may command him anything

Bid me to live, and I will live
Thy Protestant to be;
Or bid me love, and I will give
A loving heart to thee.

A heart as soft, a heart as kind,
A heart as sound and free,
As in the whole world thou canst find,
That heart I'll give to thee.

Bid that heart stay, and it will stay
To honour thy Decree;
Or bid it languish quite away,
And't shall do so for thee.

Bid me to weep, and I will weep,
While I have eyes to see;
And having none, yet I will keep
A heart to weep for thee.

Bid me despaire, and I'll despaire
Under that Cypresse tree:
Or bid me die, and I will dare
E'en Death to die for thee.

Thou art my life, my love, my heart,
The very eyes of me;
And hast command of every part,
To live and die for thee.

Robert Herrick

To Electra

I dare not ask a kiss,
I dare not beg a smile,
Lest having that, or this,
I might grow proud the while.

No, no, the utmost share
Of my desire shall be,
Only to kiss that air,
That lately kissèd thee.

Robert Herrick

The Rock Of Rubies: And The Quarrie Of Pearls

Some ask'd me where the Rubies grew?
And nothing did I say,
But with my finger pointed to
The lips of Julia.

Some ask'd how Pearls did grow, and where?
Then spoke I to my Girle,
To part her lips and shew'd them there
The Quarelets of Pearl.

One asked me where the roses grew;
I bade him not go seek,
But forthwith bade my Julia show
A bud in either cheek.

Robert Herrick

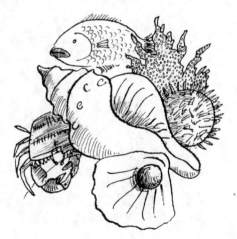

Upon The Nipples Of Julia's Breast

Have ye beheld (with much delight)
A red-rose peeping through a white?
Or else a cherry (double grac'd)
Within a lillie? Centre plac'd?
Or ever mark'd the pretty beam,
A strawberry shewes, halfe drown'd in cream?
Or seen rich rubies blushing through
A pure smooth pearl, and Orient too?
So like to this, nay all the rest,
Is each neat niplet of her breast.

Robert Herrick

Upon Julia's Clothes

When as in silks my Julia goes,
Then, then (me thinks) how sweetly flowes
The liquefaction of her clothes.

Next, when I cast mine eyes and see
That brave vibration each way free,
O how that glittering taketh me!

Robert Herrick

I Love Thee

I love thee - I love thee!
'Tis all that I can say;
It is my vision in the night,
My dreaming in the day;
The very echo of my heart,
The blessing when I pray.
I love thee - I love thee!

I love thee - I love thee!
Is ever on my tongue.
In all my proudest poesy
That chorus still is sung;
It is the verdict of my eyes
Amidst the gay and young:
I love thee - I love thee!
A thousand maids among.

I love thee - I love thee!
Thy bright and hazel glance,
The mellow lute upon those lips,
Whose tender tones entrance.
But most dear heart of hearts, thy proofs.
That still these words enhance!
I love thee - I love thee!
Whatever be thy chance.

Thomas Hood

The Time Of Roses

It was not in the winter
Our loving lot was cast;
It was the Time of Roses ‑
We pluck'd them as we pass'd!

'Twas twilight, and I bade you go,
But still you held me fast;
It was the Time of Roses ‑
We pluck'd them as we pass'd!

What else could peer thy glowing cheek,
That tears began to stud?
And when I ask'd the like of Love
You snatch'd a damask bud,

And oped it to the dainty core,
Still glowing to the last;
It was the Time of Roses ‑
We pluck'd them as we pass'd!

Thomas Hood

Ruth

She stood breast high amid the corn,
Clasped by the golden light of morn,
Like the sweetheart of the sun,
Who many a glowing kiss had won.

On her cheek an autumn flush,
Deeply ripened; such a blush
In the midst of brown was born,
Like red poppies grown with corn.

Round her eyes her tresses fell,
Which were blackest none could tell,
But long lashes veiled a light,
That had else been all too bright.

And her hat, with shady brim,
Made her tressy forehead dim ·
Thus she stood amid the stooks,
Praising God with sweetest looks:

Sure, I said, heaven did not mean,
Where I reap thou shouldst but glean,
Lay they sheaf adown and come,
Share my harvest and my home.

Thomas Hood

Only We

Dream no more that grief and pain
Could such hearts as ours enchain,
Safe from loss and safe from gain,
    Free, as love makes free.

When false friends pass coldly by,
Sigh, in earnest pity, sigh,
Turning thine unclouded eye
    Up from them to me.

Hear not danger's trampling feet
Feel not sorrow's wintry sleet
Trust that life is just and meet,
    With mine arm round thee.

Lip on lip, and eye to eye,
Love to love, we live, we die;
No more thou, and no more I,
    We, and only we!

Richard Monckton Milnes, Lord Houghton

A Une Femme

Enfant! si j'étais roi, je donnerais l'empire,
Et mon char, et mon sceptre, et mon peuple à genoux,
Et ma couronne d'or, et mes bains de porphyre,
Et mes flottes, à qui la mer ne peut suffire,
    Pour un regard de vous!

Si j'étais Dieu, la terre et l'air avec les ondes,
Les anges, les démons courbés devant ma loi,
Et le profond chaos aux entrailles fécondes
L'éternité, l'espace, et les cieux, et les mondes,
    Pour un baiser de toi!

Victor Hugo

To Celia

Drink to me, only, with thine eyes,
And I will pledge with mine;
Or leave a kiss but in the cup
And I'll not look for wine.
The thirst that from the soul doth rise
Doth ask a drink divine;
But might I of Jove's nectar sup
I would not change for thine.

I sent thee late a rosy wreath,
Not so much honouring thee
As giving it a hope, that there
It could not wither'd be;
But thou thereon did'st only breath
And sent'st it back to me;
Since when it grows, and smells, I swear,
Not of itself, but thee.

Ben Jonson

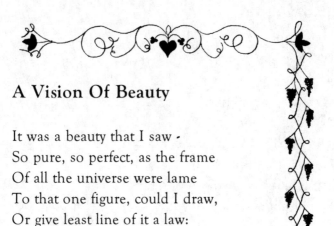

A Vision Of Beauty

It was a beauty that I saw -
So pure, so perfect, as the frame
Of all the universe were lame
To that one figure, could I draw,
Or give least line of it a law:
A skein of silk without a knot !
A fair march made without a halt!
A curious form without a fault !
A printed book without a blot!
All beauty! - and without a spot.

Ben Jonson

Those Eyes

Ah! do not wanton with those eyes,
Lest I be sick with seeing ·
Nor cast them down, but let them rise,
Lest shame destroy their being.

Ah! be not angry with those fires,
For then their threats will kill me;
Nor look too kind on my desires,
For then my hopes will spill me.

Ah! do not steep them in thy tears,
For so will sorrow slay me;
Nor spread them as distraught with fears ·
Mine own enough betray me.

Ben Jonson

Sonnet

Bright star, would I were stedfast as thou art ⁃
Not in lone splendour hung aloft the night
And watching, with eternal lids apart,
Like nature's patient, sleepless Eremite,
The moving waters at their priestlike task
Of pure ablution round earth's human shores,
Or gazing on the new soft fallen mask
Of snow upon the mountains and the moors ⁃
No ⁃ yet still stedfast, still unchangeable,
Pillow'd upon my fair love's ripening breast,
To feel forever its soft fall and swell,
Awake forever in a sweet unrest,
Still, still to hear her tender-taken breath,
And so live ever ⁃ or else swoon to death.

John Keats

To Fanny

I cry your mercy - pity - love! - ay, love! -
Merciful love that tantalizes not,
One-thoughted, never-wandering, guileless love,
Unmask'd, and being seen - without a blot!
O! let me have thee whole - all - all - be mine!
That shape, that fairness, that sweet minor zest
Of love, your kiss - those hands, those eyes divine,
That warm, white, lucent, million-pleasured breast -
Yourself - your soul - in pity give me all,
Withhold no atom's atom or I die,
Or living on perhaps, your wretched thrall,
Forget, in the midst of idle misery,
Life's purposes - the palate of my mind
Losing its gust, and my ambition blind!

John Keats

Love's Pursuit

Turn I my looks unto the skies,
Love with his arrows wounds mine eyes:
If so I gaze upon the ground,
Love then in every flower is found:
Search I the shade to fly my pain,
He meets me in the shade again:
Wend I to walk in secret grove,
Ev'n there I melt with sacred Love:
If so I bain me in the spring,
Ev'n on the brink I hear him sing:
If so I meditate alone,
He will be partner of my moan:
If so I mourn, he weeps with me,
And where I am, there will he be.
When as I talk of Rosalind,
The god from coyness waxeth kind,
And seems in selfsame flames to fry,
Because he loves as well as I;
Sweet Rosalind, for pity, rue!
For why than love I am more true:
He, if he speed, will quickly fly;
But in thy love I live and die.

Thomas Lodge

From Doctor Faustus

Was this the face that launched a thousand ships
And burnt the topless towers of Ilium?
Sweet Helen, make me immortal with a kiss.
Her lips suck forth my soul · see where it flies!
Come, Helen, come, give me my soul again.
Here will I dwell, for heaven is in these lips
And all is dross that is not Helena.
I will be Paris, and for love of thee
Instead of Troy shall Wittenberg be sack'd,
And I will combat with weak Menelaus,
And wear thy colours on my plumèd crest:
Yea, I will wound Achillis in the heel,
And then return to Helen for a kiss.
O thou art fairer than the evening air,
Clad in the beauty of a thousand stars!
Brighter art thou than flaming Jupiter,
When he appear'd to hapless Semele,
More lovely than the monarch of the sky
In wanton Arethusa's azur'd arms,
And none but thou shalt be my paramour!

Christopher Marlowe

The Passionate Shepherd To His Love

Come live with me and be my love,
And we will all the pleasures prove
That valleys, groves, hills and fields,
Or Woods or steepy mountain yields.

And we will sit upon the rocks,
And see the shepherds feed their flocks
By shallow rivers, to whose falls
Melodious birds sing madrigals.

And I will make thee beds of roses
And a thousand fragrant posies;
A cap of flowers, and a kirtle
Embroidered all with leaves of myrtle.

A gown made of the finest wool
Which from our pretty lambs we pull;
Fair linèd slippers for the cold,
With buckles of the purest gold.

A belt of straw and ivy-buds
With coral clasps and amber studs:
And if these pleasures may thee move,
Come and live with me and be my love.

Thy shepherd swains shall dance and sing
For thy delight each May morning:
If these delights thy mind may move,
Then live with me and be my love.

Christopher Marlowe

To His Coy Mistress

Had we but World enough, and Time,
This Coyness, Lady were no Crime.
We would sit down and think which way
To walk and pass our long Love's Day.
Thou by the Indian Ganges' side
Should'st Rubies find: I by the Tide
Of Humber would complain. I would
Love you ten years before the Flood:
And you should, if you please refuse
Till the conversion of the Jews.
My vegetable Love should grow
Vaster than Empires, and more slow;
An hundred years should go to praise
Thine Eyes and on thy Forehead gaze;
Two hundred to adore each Breast;
But thirty thousand to the rest;
An Age at least to every part,
And the last Age should show your Heart.
For, Lady, you deserve this State;
Nor would I love at lower rate.
But at my back I alwaies hear
Time's wingèd Chariot hurrying near;
And yonder all before us lye
Deserts of vast Eternity
Thy Beauty shall no more be found,
Nor, in thy marble Vault, shall sound
My echoing Song: then Worms shall try
That long preserved Virginity,
And your quaint Honour turn to Dust

And into Ashes all my Lust:
The Grave's a fine and private place,
But none I think, do there embrace.
Now therefore, while the youthful Hew
Sits on thy Skin like morning Dew,
And while thy willing Soul transpires
At every Pore with instant Fires,
Now let us sport us while we may;
And now, like amorous Birds of prey,
Rather at once our Time devour
Than languish in his slow-chapt power.
Let us roll all our Strength and all
Our Sweetness up, into one Ball,
And tear our Pleasures with rough strife
Thorough the Iron gates of Life:
Thus, though we cannot make our Sun
Stand still, yet we will make him run.

Andrew Marvell

It Is The Season Of The Sweet Wild Rose

It is the season of the sweet wild rose,
My Lady's emblem in the heart of me!
So golden-crownëd shines she gloriously
And with that softest dream of blood she glows:
Mild as an evening heaven round Hesper bright!
I pluck the flower, and smell it, and revive
The time when in her eyes I stood alive.
I seem to look upon it out of Night.
Here's Madam, stepping hastily. Her whims
Bid her demand the flower, which I let drop.
As I proceed, I feel her sharply stop,
And crush it under heel with trembling limbs.
She joins me in a cat-like way, and talks
Of company, and even condescends
To utter laughing scandal of old friends.
These are the summer days, and these our walks.

George Meredith

When I Would Image

When I would image her features,
Comes up a shrouded head:
I touch the outlines, shrinking;
She seems of the wandering dead.

But when love asks for nothing,
And lies on his bed of snow,
The face slips under my eyelids,
All in its living glow.

Like a dark cathedral city,
Whose spires, and domes, and towers
Quiver in violet lightnings,
My soul basks on for hours.

George Meredith

from Paradise Lost

With thee conversing I forget all time,
All seasons and their change, all please alike.
Sweet is the breath of morn, her rising sweet,
With charm of earliest birds; pleasant the sun
When first on this delightful land he spreads
His orient beams, on herb, tree, fruit, and flower,
Glistring with dew; fragrant the fertile earth
After soft showers; and sweet the coming on
Of grateful evening mild, then silent night
With this her solemn bird and this fair moon,
And these the gems of heav'n, her starry train:
But neither breath of morn when she ascends
With charm of earliest birds, nor rising sun
On this delightful land, nor herb, fruit, flower,
Glistring with dew, nor fragrance after showers,
Nor grateful evening mild, nor silent night
With this her solemn bird, nor walk by moon,
Or glittering starlight without thee is sweet.

John Milton

The Monopolist

If I were yonder wave, my dear,
And thou the isle it clasps around,
I would not let a foot come near
My land of bliss, my fairy ground!

If I were yonder conch of gold,
And thou the pearl within it placed,
I would not let an eye behold
The sacred gem my arms embraced!

If I were yonder orange tree,
And thou the blossom blooming there,
I would not yield a breath of thee,
To scent the most imploring air!

Thomas Moore

When I Loved You

When I loved you, I can't but allow
I had many an exquisite minute;
But the scorn that I feel for you now
Hath even more luxury in it!

Thus, whether we're on or we're off
Some witchery seems to await you;
To love you is pleasant enough,
But oh! 'tis delicious to hate you!

Thomas Moore

Oh, No - Not Ev'n When We First Lov'd

Oh, no - not ev'n when first we lov'd
Wert thou as dear as now thou art;
Thy beauty then my senses mov'd
But now thy virtues bind my heart.
What was but Passion's sigh before
Has since been turn'd to Reason's vow;
And, though I then might love thee more,
Trust me, I love thee better now.

Although my heart in earlier youth
Might kindle with more wild desire,
Believe me, it has gain'd in truth
Much more than it has lost in fire.
The flame now warms my inmost core
That then but sparkled o'er my brow
And though I seem'd to love thee more
Yet, oh, I love thee better now.

Thomas Moore

Across The Sky

Across the sky the daylight crept,
And birds grew garrulous in the grove,
And on my marriage-morn I slept
A soft sleep undisturb'd by love.

Coventry Patmore

A Farewell

With all my will, but much against my heart,
We two now part.
My very dear,
Our solace is, the sad road lies so clear.
It needs no art,
With faint, averted feet
And many a tear,
In our opposed paths to persevere.
Go thou to east, I west.
We will not say
There's any hope, it is so far away.
But, O, my best,
When the one darling of our widowhead,
The nursling Grief,
Is dead,
And no dews blur our eyes
To see the peach-bloom come in evening skies,
Perchance we may,
Where now this night is day,
And even through faith of still averted feet,
Making full circle of our banishment,
Amazed meet;
The bitter journey to the bourne so sweet
Seasoning the termless feast of our content
With tears of recognition never dry.

Coventry Patmore

To Helen

Helen, thy beauty is to me
Like those Nicèan barks of yore
That gently, o'er a perfumed sea
The weary way-worn wanderer bore
To his own native shore.

On desperate seas long wont to roam,
Thy hyacinth hair, thy classic face,
Thy Naiad airs have brought me home
To the glory that was Greece,
And the grandeur that was Rome.

Lo, in yon brilliant window-niche
How statue-like I see thee stand,
The agate lamp within thy hand,
Ah! Psyche, from the regions which
Are holy-land!

Edgar Allan Poe

To One In Paradise

Thou wast all that to me, love,
For which my soul did pine:
A green isle in the sea, love,
A fountain and a shrine
All wreathed with fairy fruits and flowers,
And all the flowers were mine.

Ah, dream too bright to last:
Ah, starry Hope, that didst arise
But to be overcast!
A voice from out the Future cries,
"On! on!" - but o'er the Past
(Dim gulf) my spirit hovering lies
Mute, motionless, aghast.

For, alas! alas! with me
The light of Life is o'er!
No more - no more - no more -
(Such language holds the solemn sea
To the sands upon the shore!)
Shall bloom the thunder-blasted tree,
Or the stricken eagle soar.

And all my days are trances,
And all my nightly dreams
Are where thy dark eye glances,
And where thy footstep gleams -
In what ethereal dances,
By what eternal streams.

Edgar Allan Poe

Now What is Love?

Now what is love, I pray thee, tell?
It is that fountain and that well
Where pleasure and repentance dwell;
It is, perhaps, the saucing bell
That tolls all into heaven or hell;
And this is love, as I hear tell.

Yet what is love, I prithee, say?
It is a work on holiday,
It is December matched with May,
When lusty bloods in fresh array
Hear ten months after of the play;
And this is love, as I hear say.

Yet what is love, good shepherd, sain?
It is a sunshine mixed with rain,
It is a toothache or like pain,
It is a game where none hath gain;
The lass saith no, yet would full fain;
And this is love, as I hear sain.

Yet, shepherd, what is love, I pray?
It is a yes, it is a nay,
A pretty kind of sporting fray,
It is a thing will soon away.
Then, nymphs, take vantage while ye may;
And this is love, as I hear say.

Yet what is love, good shepherd, show?
A thing that creeps, it cannot go,
A prize that passeth to and fro,
A thing for one, a thing for moe,
And he that proves shall find it so;
And shepherd, this is love, I trow.

Sir Walter Raleigh

The Nymph's Reply To The Shepherd

If all the world and love were young,
And truth in every shepherd's tongue,
These pretty pleasures might me move
To live with thee and be thy love.

But Time drives flocks from field to fold;
When rivers rage and rocks grow cold;
And Philomel becometh dumb;
The rest complains of cares to come.

The flowers do fade, and wanton fields
To wayward Winter reckoning yields:
A honey tongue, a heart of gall,
Is fancy's spring, but sorrow's fall.

Thy gowns, thy shoes, thy beds of roses,
Thy cap, thy kirtle, and thy posies,
Soon break, soon wither, soon forgotten -
In folly ripe, in reason rotten.

Thy belt of straw and ivy - buds,
Thy coral clasps and amber studs -
All these in me no means can move
To come to thee and be thy love.

But could youth last, and love still breed,
Had joys no date, nor age no need,
Then these delights my mind might move
To live with thee and be thy love.

Sir Walter Raleigh

Sonnet

I wish I could remember that first day,
First hour, first moment of your meeting me,
If bright or dim the season, it might be
Summer or Winter for aught I can say;
So unrecorded did it slip away,
So blind was I to see and to foresee,
So dull to mark the budding of my tree
That would not blossom yet for many a May.
If only I could recollect it, such
A day of days! I let it come and go
As traceless as a thaw of bygone snow;
It seemed to mean so little, meant so much;
If only now I could recall that touch,
First touch of hand in hand - Did one but know!

Christina Rossetti

Sonnet

O my heart's heart and you who are to me
More than myself myself, God be with you,
Keep you in strong obedience, leal and true
To him whose noble service setteth free,
Give you all good we see or can foresee,
Make your joys many and your sorrows few,
Bless you in what you bear and what you do,
Yea, perfect you as He would have you be.
So much for you; but what for me dear friend?
To love you without stint and all I can
Today, tomorrow, world without an end:
To love you much, and yet to love you more,
As Jordan at its flood sweeps either shore;
Since woman is the helpmeet made for man.

Christina Rossetti

Echo

Come to me in the silence of the night;
Come in the speaking silence of a dream;
Come with soft rounded cheeks and eyes as bright
As sunlight on a stream;
Come back in tears;
O memory, hope, love of finished years.

O dream how sweet, too sweet, too bitter sweet
Whose wakening should have been in Paradise,
Where souls brimful of love abide and meet ;
Where thirsting longing eyes
Watch the slow door
That, opening, letting in, lets out no more.

Yet come to me in dreams; that I may live
My very life again though cold in death:
Come back to me in dreams, that I may give
Pulse for pulse, breath for breath:
Speak low, lean low,
As long ago, my love, how long ago?

Christina Rossetti

Remember

Remember me when I am gone away,
Gone far away into the silent land;
When you can no more hold me by the hand
Nor I half turn to go, yet turning stay.
Remember me when no more day by day
You tell me of our future that you planned;
Only remember me; you understand
It will be late to counsel then or pray.
Yet if you should forget me for a while
And afterwards remember, do not grieve:
For if the darkness and corruption leave
A vestige of thought that once I had,
Better by far you should forget and smile
Than you should remember and be sad.

Christina Rossetti

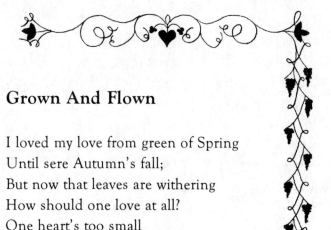

Grown And Flown

I loved my love from green of Spring
Until sere Autumn's fall;
But now that leaves are withering
How should one love at all?
One heart's too small
For hunger, cold, love, everything.

I loved my love on sunny days
Until late Summer's wane;
But now that frost begins to glaze
How should one love again?
Nay, love and pain
Walk wide apart in diverse ways.

I loved my love - alas to see
That this should be, alas!
I thought that this could scarcely be,
Yet has it come to pass:
Sweet sweet love was,
Now bitter bitter grown to me.

Christina Rossetti

Sonnet

Youth gone, and beauty gone if ever there
Dwelt beauty in so poor a face as this;
Youth gone and beauty, what remains of bliss?
I will not bind fresh roses in my hair,
To shame a cheek at best but little fair ‑
Leave youth his roses, who can bear a thorn ‑
I will not seek for blossoms anywhere,
Except such common flowers as blow with corn.
Youth gone and beauty gone, what doth remain?
The longing of a heart pent up forlorn,
A silent heart whose silence loves and longs;
The silence of a heart which sang its songs
While youth and beauty made a summer morn,
Silence of love that cannot sing again.

Christina Rossetti

An End

Love, strong as Death, is dead.
Come, let us make his bed
Among the dying flowers:
A green turf at his head;
And a stone at his feet,
Whereon we may sit
In the quiet evening hours.

He was born in the Spring,
And died before the harvesting:
On the last warm Summer day
He left us; he would not stay
For Autumn twilight cold and grey.
Sit we by his grave, and sing
He is gone away.

To few chords and sad and low
Sing we so:
Be our eyes fixed on the grass
Shadow-veiled as the years pass,
While we think of all that was
In the long ago.

Christina Rossetti

Song

When I am dead, my dearest,
Sing no sad songs for me;
Plant thou no roses at my head,
Nor shady cypress tree:
Be the green grass above me
With showers and dewdrops wet;
And if thou wilt, remember,
And if thou wilt, forget.
I shall not see the shadows,
I shall not feel the rain;
I shall not hear the nightingale
Sing on, as if in pain;
And dreaming through the twilight
That doth not rise nor set,
Haply I may remember,
And haply may forget.

Christina Rossetti

Even So

So it is, my dear.
All such things touch secret strings
For heavy hearts to hear.
So it is, my dear.

Very like indeed:
Sea and sky, afar, on high,
Sand and strewn seaweed ·
Very like indeed.

But the sea stands spread
As one wall with the flat skies,
Where the lean black craft like flies
Seem well-nigh stagnated,
Soon to drop off dead.

Seemed it so to us
When I was thine and thou wast mine,
And all these things were thus,
But all our world in us?

Could we be so now?
Not if all beneath heaven's pall
Lay dead but I and thou,
Could we be so now!

Dante Gabriel Rossetti

Sudden Light

I have been here before,
But when or how I cannot tell:
I know the grass beyond the door,
The sweet keen smell,
The sighing sound, the lights around the shore.

You have been mine before -
How long ago I may not know:
But just when at that swallow's soar
Your neck turned so,
Some veil did fall,-I knew it all of yore.

Has this been thus before?
And shall not thus time's eddying flight
Still with our lives our love restore
In death's despite
And day and night yield one delight once more?

Dante Gabriel Rossetti

Silent Noon

Your hands lie open in the long fresh grass,
The finger-points look through like rosy blooms;
Your eyes smile peace. The pasture gleams and glooms
'Neath billowing skies that scatter and amass.
All round our nest, far as the eye can pass,
Are golden kingcup-fields with silver edge
Where the cow-parsley skirts the hawthorn-hedge.
'Tis visible silence still as the hourglass.
Deep n the sun-searched growths the dragonfly
Hangs like a blue thread loosened from the sky.
So this winged hour is dropt to us from above
Oh! clasp we to our hearts, for deathless dower,
This close-companioned inarticulate hour
When twofold silence was the song of love.

Dante Gabriel Rossetti

Willowwood

I sat with Love upon a woodside well,
Leaning across the water, I and he;
Nor ever did he speak nor looked at me,
But touched his lute wherein was audible
The certain secret thing he had to tell:
Only our mirrored eyes met silently
In the low wave; and that sound seemed to be
The passionate voice I knew; and my tears fell.

And at their fall, his eyes beneath grew hers;
And with his foot and with his wing feathers
He swept the spring that watered my heart's drouth.
Then the dark ripples spread to waving hair,
And as I stopped, her own lips rising there
Bubbled with brimming kisses at my mouth.

Dante Gabriel Rossetti

Love As The Theme Of Poets

And said I that my limbs were old;
And said I that my blood was cold,
And that my kindly fire was fled,
And my poor withered heart was dead,
And that I might not sing of love?
How could I to the dearest theme,
That ever warmed a minstrel's dream
So foul, so false, a recreant prove!
How could I name love's very name
Nor wake my harp to notes of flame!

In peace, Love tunes the shepherd's reed;
In war, he mounts the warrior's steed;
In halls, in gay attire is seen;
In hamlets, dances on the green.
Love rules the court, the camp, the grove,
And men below, and saints above;
For love is heaven, and heaven is love.

Sir Walter Scott

An Hour With Thee

An hour with thee! When earliest day
Dapples with gold the eastern grey,
Oh, what can frame my mind to bear
The toil and turmoil, cark and care,
New griefs, which coming hours unfold,
And sad remembrance of the old?
One hour with thee.

One hour with thee! When burning June
Waves his red flag at pitch of noon;
What shall repay the faithful swain,
His labour on the sultry plain;
And, more than cave or sheltering bough
Cool feverish blood and throbbing brow?
One hour with thee.

One hour with thee! When sun is set,
Oh, what can teach me to forget
The thankless labours of the day;
The hopes, the wishes, flung away;
The increasing wants, and lessening gains,
The master's pride, who scorns my pains?
One hour with thee.

Sir Walter Scott

Love And The Rose

The rose is fairest when 'tis budding new,
And hope is brightest when it dawns from fears:
The rose is sweetest wash'd with morning dew,
And love is loveliest when embalm'd in tears.
O wilding rose, whom fancy thus endears,
I bid your blossoms in my bonnet wave,
Emblem of hope and love through future years!
Thus spoke young Norman, heir of Armandare
What time the sun arose on Vennachar's broad wave.

Sir Walter Scott

To Cloris

Cloris, I cannot say your eyes
Did my unwary heart surprise;
Nor will I swear it was your face,
Your shape, or any nameless grace:
For you are so entirely fair,
To love a part, injustice were;
No drowning man can know which drop
Of water his last breath did stop;
So when the stars in heaven appear,
And join to make the night look clear;
The light we no one's bounty call,
But the obliging gift of all.
He that does lips or hands adore,
Deserves them only, and no more;
But I love all, and every part,
And nothing less can ease my heart.
Cupid, that lover, weakly strikes,
Who can express what 'tis he likes.

Sir Charles Sedley

Sonnet

That time of year thou may'st in me behold
When yellow leaves, or none, or few, do hang
Upon those boughs which shake against the cold,
Bare ruined choirs, where late the sweet birds sang.
In me thou seest the twilight of such day
As after sunset fadeth in the west;
Which by and by black night doth take away,
Death's second self, that seals up all in rest.
In me thou seest the glowing of such fire,
That on the ashes of his youth doth lie,
As the death-bed whereon it must expire,
Consumed with that which it was nourished by.
  This thou perceiv'st, which makes thy love more
strong,
  To love that well which thou must leave ere long.

William Shakespeare

Sonnet

My love is strengthen'd, though more weak in
  seeming;
I love not less, thou less the show appear;
That love is merchandiz'd whose rich esteeming
The owner's tongue doth publish everywhere.
Our love was new, and then but in the spring,
When I was won't to greet it with my lays;
As Philomel in summer's front doth sing
And stops her pipe in growth of riper days:
Not that the summer is less pleasant now
Than when her mournful hymns did hush the night,
But that wild music burthens every bough,
And sweets grown common lose their dear delight.
  Therefore, like her, I sometime hold my
tongue,
  Because I would not dull you with my song.

William Shakespeare

Sonnet

Let me not to the marriage of true minds
Admit impediments. Love is not love
Which alters when it alteration finds,
Or bends with the remover to remove:
O, no; it is an ever-fixed mark,
That looks on tempests and is never shaken;
It is the star to every wandering bark,
Whose worth's unknown, although his height be
  taken.
Love's not Time's fool, though rosy lips and cheeks
Within his bending sickle's compass come;
Love alters not with his brief hours and weeks,
But bears it out even to the edge of doom.
  If this be error and upon me prov'd,
  I never writ, nor no man ever lov'd.

William Shakespeare

Sonnet

Lord of my love, to whom in vassalage
Thy merit hath my duty strongly knit.
To thee I send this written embassage,
To witness duty, not to show my wit:
Duty so great, which wit so poor as mine
May make seem bare, in wanting words to show it,
But that I hope some good conceit of thine
In thy soul's thought, all naked, will bestow it
Till whatsoever star that guides my moving,
Points on me graciously with fair aspect,
And puts apparel on my tatter'd loving,
To show me worthy of thy sweet respect:
  Then may I dare to boast how I do love thee;
  Till then not show my head where thou mayst
prove me.

William Shakespeare

Sonnet

Thus can my love excuse the slow offense
Of my dull bearer when from thee I speed:
From where thou art why should I haste me thence?
Till I return, of posting is no need.
O, what excuse will my poor beast then find,
When swift extremity can seem but slow?
Then should I spur, though mounted on the wind,
In winged speed no motion shall I know:
Then can no horse with my desire keep pace;
Therefore desire, of perfect'st love being made
Shall neigh - no dull flesh - in his fiery race;
But love, for love, thus shall excuse my jade;
  Since from thee going he went willful-slow,
  Towards thee I'll run and give him leave to go.

William Shakespeare

Sonnet

Not marble, nor the gilded monuments
Of princes, shall outlive this powerful rhyme;
But you shall shine more bright in these contents
Than unswept stone, besmear'd with sluttish time.
When wasteful war shall statues overturn,
And broils root out the work of masonry,
Nor Mars his sword nor war's quick fire shall burn
The living record of your memory.
'Gainst death and all-oblivious enmity
Shall you pace forth; your praise shall still find room
Even in the eyes of all posterity
That wear this world out to the ending doom.
  So, till the judgement that yourself arise,
   You live in this, and dwell in lovers' eyes.

William Shakespeare

Sonnet

So are you to my thoughts as food to life,
Or as sweet-season'd showers are to the ground;
And for the peace of you I hold such strife
As 'twixt a miser and his wealth is found;
Now proud as an enjoyer, and anon
Doubting the filching age will steal his treasure;
Now counting best to be with you alone,
Then better'd that the world may see my pleasure:
Sometime all full with feasting on your sight,
And by and by clean starved for a look;
Possessing or pursuing no delight,
Save what is had or must from you be took.
  Thus do I pine and surfeit day by day,
   Or gluttoning on all, or all away.

William Shakespeare

Sonnet

Not from the stars do I my judgement pluck;
And yet methinks I have astronomy,
But not to tell of good or evil luck,
Of plagues, of dearths, or seasons' quality;
Nor can I fortune to brief minutes tell,
Pointing to each his thunder, rain and wind,
Or say with princes if it shall go well,
By oft predict that I in heaven find:
But from thine eyes my knowledge I derive,
And, constant stars, in them I read such art,
As truth and beauty shall together thrive,
If from thyself to store thou wouldst convert;
  Or else of thee this I prognosticate:
  Thy end is truth's and beauty's doom and date.

William Shakespeare

Sonnet

Some glory in their birth, some in their skill,
Some in their wealth, some in their body's force,
Some in their garments, though new-fangled ill;
Some in their hawks and hounds, some in their
  horse;
And every humour hath his adjunct pleasure,
Wherein it finds a joy above the rest:
But these particulars are not my measure;
All these I better in one general best.
Thy love is better than high birth to me,
Richer than wealth, prouder than garments cost,
Of more delight than hawks and horses be;
And, having thee, of all men's pride I boast:
  Wretched in this alone, that thou mayst take
  All this away and me most wretched make.

William Shakespeare

Sonnet

Shall I compare thee to a summer's day?
Thou art more lovely and more temperate:
Rough winds do shake the darling buds of May,
And summer's lease hath all too short a date:
Sometime too hot the eye of heaven shines,
And often is his gold complexion dimm'd;
And every fair from fair sometime declines,
By chance or nature's changing course untrimm'd;
But thy eternal summer shall not fade,
Nor lose possession of that fair thou ow'st;
Nor shall Death brag thou wander'st in his shade,
When in eternal lines to time thou grow'st;
  So long as men can breathe, or eyes can see,
  So long lives this, and this gives life to thee.

William Shakespeare

Sonnet

When in the chronicle of wasted time
I see descriptions of the fairest wights,
And beauty making beautiful old rhyme
In praise of ladies dead and lovely knights,
Then in the blazon of sweet beauty's best,
Of hand, of foot, of lip, of eye, of brow,
I see their antique pen would have express'd
Even such a beauty as you master now.
So all their praises are but prophecies
Of this our time, all you prefiguring;
And, for they look'd but with divining eyes
They had not skill enough your worth to sing:
  For we, which now behold these present days,
  Have eyes to wonder, but lack tongues to praise.

William Shakespeare

Sonnet

That thou hast her, it is not all my grief,
And yet it may be said I lov'd her dearly;
That she hath thee, is of my wailing chief,
A loss in love that touches me more nearly.
Loving offenders, thus I will excuse ye:
Thou dost love her, because thou knew'st I love her;
And for my sake even so doth she abuse me
Suffering my friend for my sake to approve her.
If I lose thee, my loss is my love's gain,
And losing her, my friend hath found that loss;
Both and each other, and I lose both twain
And both for my sake lay on me this cross:
  But here's the joy; my friend and I are one;
  Sweet flattery! then she loves but me alone.

William Shakespeare

Sonnet

Farewell! thou art too dear for my possessing,
And like enough thou know'st thy estimate:
The charter of thy worth gives thee releasing;
My bonds in thee are all determinate.
For how do I hold thee but by thy granting?
And for that riches where is my deserving?
The cause of this fair gift in me is wanting,
And so my patent back again is swerving.
Thyself thou gav'st, thy own worth then not knowing,
Or me, to whom thou gav'st it, else mistaking;
So thy great gift, upon misprision growing,
Comes home again, on better judgement making.
  Thus have I had thee, as a dream doth flatter,
  In sleep a king, but waking no such matter.

William Shakespeare

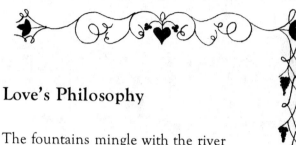

Love's Philosophy

The fountains mingle with the river
And the rivers with the Ocean,
The winds of Heaven mix for ever
With a sweet emotion;
Nothing in the world is single;
All things by a law divine
In one spirit meet and mingle.
Why not I with thine? -

See the mountains kiss high Heaven
And the waves clasp one another;
No sister-flower would be forgiven
If it disdained its brother;
And the sunlight clasps the earth
And the moonbeams kiss the sea:
What is all this sweet work worth
If thou kiss not me?

Percy Bysshe Shelley

I Arise From Dreams Of Thee

I arise from dreams of thee
In the first sweet sleep of night,
When the winds are breathing low,
And the stars are shining bright.
I arise from dreams of thee,
And a spirit in my feet
Hath led me - who knows how? -
To thy chamber window, Sweet!

The wandering airs they faint
On the dark, the silent stream -
The Champak odours fail
Like sweet thoughts in a dream;
The nightingale's complaint,
It dies upon her heart,
As I must die on thine,
O, beloved as thou art!

O, lift me from the grass!
I die, I faint!, I fail!
Let thy love in kisses rain
On my lips and eyelids pale.
My cheek is cold and white, alas!
My heart beats loud and fast:
Oh! press it close to thine again,
Where it will break at last.

Percy Bysshe Shelley

The Summit

Our breath shall intermix, our bosoms bound,
And our veins beat together; and our lips,
With other eloquence than words, eclipse
The soul that burns between them; and the wells
Which boil under our being's inmost cells
The fountains of our deepest life, shall be
Confused in passion's golden purity
As mountain springs under the morning sun.
We shall become the same, we shall be one
Spirit within two frames, oh, wherefore two?
One passion in twin hearts, which grows and grew
Till, like two meteors of expanding flame,
Those spheres instinct with it become the same,
Touch, mingle, are transfigured; ever still
Burning, yet ever inconsumable;
In one another's substance finding food
Light flames too pure and light and unimbued
To nourish their bright lives with baser prey,
Which point to heaven and cannot pass away :
One hope within two wills, one will beneath
Two overshadowing minds, one life, one death,
One heaven, one hell, one immortality,
And one annihilation!

Percy Bysshe Shelley

From The Arabic: An Imitation

My faint spirit was sitting in the light
Of thy looks, my love;
It panted for thee like the hind at noon
For the brooks, my love.
The barb whose hoofs outspeed the tempest's flight
Bore thee far from me;
My heart, for my weak feet were weary soon,
Did companion thee.

Ah! fleeter far than fleetest storm or steed,
Or the death they bear,
The heart which tender thought clothes like a dove
With the wings of care;
In the battle, in the darkness, in the need,
Shall mine cling to thee,
Nor claim one smile for all the comfort, love,
It may bring to thee.

Percy Bysshe Shelley

When Passion's Trance Is Overpast

When passion's trance is overpast,
If tenderness and truth could last,
Or live, whilst all wild feelings keep
Some mortal slumber, dark and deep,
I should not weep, I should not weep!

It were enough to feel, to see,
Thy soft eyes gazing tenderly,
And dream the rest - and burn and be
The secret food of fires unseen,
Couldst thou but be as thou hast been.

After the slumber of the year
The woodland violets reappear;
All things revive in field or grove,
And sky and sea, but two, which move
And form all others - life, and love.

Percy Byshhe Shelley

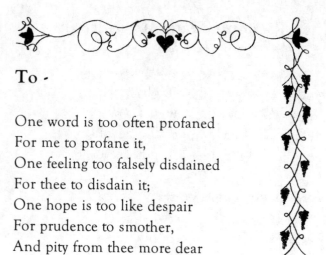

To -

One word is too often profaned
For me to profane it,
One feeling too falsely disdained
For thee to disdain it;
One hope is too like despair
For prudence to smother,
And pity from thee more dear
Than that from another.

I can give not what men call love,
But wilt thou accept not
The worship the heart lifts above
And the Heavens reject not -
The desire of the moth for the star,
Of the night for the morrow,
The devotion to something afar
From the sphere of our sorrow?

Percy Bysshe Shelley

When The Lamp Is Shattered

When the lamp is shattered
The light in the dust lies dead;
When the cloud is scattered,
The rainbow's glory is shed.
When the lute is broken,
Sweet tones are remembered not;
When the lips have spoken,
Loved accents are soon forgot.

As music and splendour
Survive not the lamp and the lute
The heart's echoes render
No song when the spirit is mute
No song but sad dirges,
Like the wind through a ruined cell,
Or the mournful surges
That ring the dead seaman's knell.

When hearts have once mingled,
Love first leaves the well-built nest;
The weak one is singled
To endure what it once possessed.
O Love! who bewailest
The frailty of all things here,
Why choose you the frailest
For your cradle, your home, and your bier?

Its passions will rock thee
As the storms rock the ravens on high;

Bright reason will mock thee
Like the sun from a wintry sky.
From thy nest every rafter
Will rot, and thine eagle home
Leave thee naked to laughter,
When leaves fall and cold winds come.

Percy Bysshe Shelley

Echoes And Memories

Music, when soft voices die,
Vibrates in the memory -
Odours, when sweet violets sicken,
Live within the sense they quicken .

Rose leaves, when the rose is dead,
Are heaped for the belovèd's bed;
And so thy thoughts, when thou art gone,
Love itself shall slumber on.

Percy Bysshe Shelley

Because I Breathe Not Love

Because I breathe not love to every one,
Nor do not use set colours for to wear,
Nor nourish special locks of vowed hair,
Nor give each speech a full point of a groan,
The courtly nymphs, acquainted with the moan:
Of them who on their lips love's standard bear:
"What, he?" say they of me. "Now I dare swear,
He cannot love; no, no, let him alone."
And think so still, so Stella know my mind.
Profess, indeed, I do not Cupid's art;
But you, fair maids, at length this true shall find,
That his right badge is but worn in the heart;
Dumb swans, not chattering pies, do lovers prove;
They love indeed, who quake to say they love.

Sir Philip Sidney

Sonnet

With how sad steps, O moon, thou climb'st the skies;
How silently, and with how wan a face.
What, may it be that even in heav'nly place
That busy archer his sharp arrows tries?
Sure, if that long-with-love-acquainted eyes
Can judge of love, thou feel'st a lover's case;
I read it in thy looks; thy languished grace
To me that feel the like, thy state descries.
Then ev'n of fellowship, O moon, tell me
Is constant love deemed there but want of wit?
Are beauties there as proud as here they be?
Do they above love to be loved, and yet
Those lovers scorn whom that love doth possess?
Do they call virtue there ungratefulness?

Sir Philip Sidney

Sonnet

Dear, why make you more of a dog than me?
If he do love, I burn, I burn in love:
If he wait well, I never thence would move:
If he be fair, yet but a dog can be.
Little he is, so little worth is he;
He barks, my songs thine own voice oft doth prove;
Bidden, perhaps he fetcheth thee a glove,
But I unbid, fetch even my soul to thee.
Yet while I languish, him that bosom clips,
That lap doth lap, nay lets, in spite of spite,
This sour-breath'd mate taste of those sugar'd lips.
Alas, if you grant only such delight
To witless things, then love I hope (since wit
Becomes a clog) will soon ease me of it.

Sir Philip Sidney

The Garden Of Beauty

Coming to kiss her lips (such grace I found),
Me seem'd I smelt a garden of sweet flow'rs
That dainty odours from them threw around,
For damsels fit to deck their lovers' bow'rs.
Her lips did smell like unto gilliflowers,
Her ruddy cheeks like unto roses red,
Her snowy brows like budded bellamoures,
Her lovely eyes like pinks but newly spread,
Her goodly bosom like a strawberry bed,
Her neck like to a bunch of cullambines,
Her breast like lilies ere their leaves be shed,
Her nipples like young blossom'd jessamines:
Such fragrant flow'rs do give most odourous smell,
But her sweet odour did them all excel.

Edmund Spenser

Love In Absence

Like as the culver on the bared bough
Sits mourning for the absence of her mate,
And in her songs sends many a wishful vow
For his return, that seems to linger late;
So I alone, now left disconsolate,
Mourn to myself the absence of my love,
And wandering here and there all desolate,
Seek with my plaints to match that mournful dove.
No joy of ought that under heaven doth hove
Can comfort me, but her own joyous sight,
Whose sweet aspect both god and man can move,
In her unspotted pleasance to delight:
Dark is my day whiles her fair light I miss,
And dead my life, that wants such lively bliss.

Edmund Spenser

My Love Is Like To Ice

My love is like to ice, and I to fire:
How comes it then that this her cold so great
Is not dissolved through my so hot desire,
But harder grows the more I her entreat!
Or how comes it that my exceeding heat
Is not allayed by her heart - frozen cold,
But that I burn much more in boiling sweat,
And feel my flames augmented manifold!
What more miraculous thing may be told
That fire, which all things melts, should harden ice,
And ice, which is congeal'd with senseless cold;
Should kindle fire by wonderful device!
Such is the power of love in gentle mind,
That it can alter all the course of kind.

Edmund Spenser

I Will Make You Brooches

I will make you brooches and toys for your delight
Of bird-song at morning and star-shine at night.
I will make a place fit for you and me
Of green days in forest and blue days at sea.

I will make my kitchen, and you shall keep your
   room,
Where white flows the river and bright blows the
   broom,
And you shall wash your linen and keep your body
   white
In rainfall at morning and dewfall at night.

And this shall be for music when no one else is
   near,
The fine song for singing, the rare song to hear!
That only I remember, that only you admire,
Of the broad road that stretches and the roadside
   fire.

Robert Louis Stevenson

My Wife

Trusty, dusky, vivid, true,
With eyes of gold and bramble-dew,
Steel-true and blade-straight,
The great artificer
Made my mate.

Honour, anger, valour, fire;
A love that life could never tire,
Death quench or evil stir,
The mighty master
Gave to her.

Teacher, tender comrade, wife,
A fellow-farer true through life,
Heart-whole and soul-free
The august father
Gave to me.

Robert Louis Stevenson

The Stolen Heart

I prythee send me back my heart
Since I cannot have thine;
For if from yours you will not part,
Why then shouldst thou have mine?

Yet now I think on't, let it lie;
To find it were in vain,
For thou'st a thief in either eye
Would steal it back again.

Why should two hearts in one breast lie,
And yet not lodge together?
O love! where is thy sympathy,
If thus our breasts you sever?

But love is such a mystery,
I cannot find it out;
For when I think I'm best resolved
I then am most in doubt.

Then farewell love, and farewell woe,
I will no longer pine;
For I'll believe I have her heart
As much as she hath mine.

Sir John Suckling

On Stella's Birthday

Stella this day is thirty-four
(We shan't dispute a year or more),
However Stella, be not troubled,
Although thy size and years are doubled,
Since first I saw thee at sixteen
The brightest virgin on the green,
So little is thy form declin'd
Made up so largely in thy mind.
Oh, would it please the Gods to split
Thy beauty, size, and years, and wit,
No age could furnish out a pair
Of nymphs so graceful, wise and fair
With half the lustre of your eyes,
With half your wit, your years and size:
And then before it grew too late,
How should I beg of gentle fate
(That either nymph might have her swain)
To split my worship too in twain.

Jonathan Swift

Kissing Her Hair

Kissing her hair, I sat against her feet:
Wove and unwove it - wound, and found it sweet;
Made fast there with her hands, drew down her eyes,
Deep as deep flowers, and dreamy like dim skies;
With her own tresses bound, and found her fair -
    Kissing her hair.

Sleep were no sweeter than her face to me -
Sleep of cold sea-bloom under the cold sea:
What pain could get between my face and hers?
What new sweet thing would Love not relish worse?
Unless, perhaps, white Death had kissed me there -
    Kissing her hair.

Algernon Charles Swinburne

Oblation

Ask nothing more of me, sweet;
All I can give you I give;
Heart of my heart, were it more,
More should be laid at your feet:
Love that should help you to live -
Song that should spur you to soar.

All things were nothing to give,
Once to have sense of you more -
Touch you and taste of you, sweet,
Think you and breathe you, and live
Swept of your wings as they soar,
Trodden by chance of your feet.

I, who have love and no more,
Bring you but love of you, sweet.
He that hath more, let him give;
He that hath wings, let him soar:
Mine is the heart at your feet
Here, that must love you to live.

Algernon Charles Swinburne

Marriage Morning

Light, so low upon earth,
You send a flash to the sun.
Here is the golden close of love,
All my wooing is done.
Oh, the woods and the meadows,
Woods where we hid from the wet,
Stiles where we stay'd to be kind
Meadows in which we met!

Light, so low in the vale,
You flash and lighten afar,
For this is the golden morning of love,
And you are his morning star.
Flash, I am coming, I come,
By meadow and stile and wood,
Oh, lighten into my eyes and heart,
Into my heart and my blood!

Heart, are you great enough
For a love that never tires?
O heart, are you great enough for love?
I have heard of thorns and briers.
Over the thorns and briers,
Over the meadows and stiles,
Over the world to the end of it
Flash for a million miles.

Alfred, Lord Tennyson

At The Church Gate

Although I enter not,
Yet round about the spot
Oft times I hover:
And near the sacred gate,
With longing eyes I wait,
Expectant of her.

The minster bell tolls out
Above the city's rout
And noise and humming
They've hushed the minster bell:
The organ 'gins to swell:
She's coming, she's coming!

My lady comes at last,
Timid, and stepping fast,
And hastening hither,
With modest eyes downcast:
She comes - she's here - she's past-
May heaven go with her!

Kneel, undisturb'd, fair saint!
Pour out your praise or plaint
Meekly and duly;
I will not enter there,
To sully your pure prayer
With thoughts unruly.

But suffer me to pace
Round the forbidden place,
Lingering a minute,
Like outcast spirits who wait
And see through heaven's gate
Angels within it.

William Makepeace Thackeray

Like The Touch of Rain

Like the touch of rain she was
On a man's flesh and hair and eyes
When the joy of walking thus
Has taken him by surprise:

With the love of the storm he burns,
He sings, he laughs, well I know how,
But forgets when he returns
As I shall not forget her 'Go now.'

Those two shut a door
Between me and the blessed rain
That was never shut before
And will not open again.

Edward Thomas

My Queen

He loves not well whose love is bold!
I would not have thee come too nigh:
The sun's gold would not seem pure gold
Unless the sun were in the sky;
To take him thence and chain him near
Would make his beauty disappear.

He keeps his state - keep thou in thine,
And shine upon me from afar!
So shall I bask in light divine,
That falls from love's own guiding star;
So shall thy eminence be high,
And so my passion shall not die.

But all my life shall reach its hands
Of lofty longing toward thy face,
And be as one who speechless stands
In rapture at some perfect grace!
My love, my hope, my all shall be
To look to heaven and look to thee!

Thy eyes shall be the heavenly lights;
Thy voice the gentle summer breeze,
What time it sways, on moonlit nights,
The murmuring tops of leafy trees;
And I shall touch thy beauteous form
In June's red roses, rich and warm.

But thou thyself shalt come not down
From that pure region far above;
But keep thy throne and wear thy crown,
Queen of my heart and queen of love!
A monarch in thy realm complete,
And I a monarch - at thy feet!

William Winter

Sonnet Upon A Stolen Kiss

Now gentle sleep hath closed up those eyes
Which, waking, kept my boldest thoughts in awe;
And free access unto that sweet lip lies,
From whence I long the rosy breath to draw.
Methinks no wrong it were, if I should steal
From those two melting rubies one poor kiss;
None sees the theft that would the theft reveal,
Nor rob I her of aught what she can miss:
Nay, should I twenty kisses take away,
There would be little sign I would do so;
Why then should I this robbery delay?
O, she may wake and therewith angry grow!
Well, if she do I'll back restore that one,
And twenty hundred thousand more for loan.

George Wither

Yes! Thou Art Fair

Yes! thou art fair, yet be not moved
To scorn the declaration,
That sometimes I in thee have loved
My fancy's own creation.

Imagination needs must stir:
Dear maid, this truth believe,
Minds that have nothing to confer
Find little to perceive.

Be pleased that nature made thee fit
To feed my heart's devotion,
By laws to which all forms submit
In sky, air, earth, and ocean.

William Wordsworth

What Heavenly Smiles!

What heavenly smiles! O Lady mine
Through my very heart they shine;
And, if my brow gives back their light,
Do thou look gladly on the sight;
As the clear Moon with modest pride
Beholds her own bright beams.
Reflected from the mountain's side
And from the headlong streams.

William Wordsworth

Among All Lovely Things

Among all lovely things my Love had been;
Had noted well the stars, all flowers that grew
About her home; but she had never seen
A Glow-worm, never one, and this I knew.

While riding near her home one stormy night
A single Glow-worm did I chance to espy;
I gave a fervent welcome to the sight,
And from my horse I leapt; great joy had I.

Upon a leaf the Glow-worm did I lay,
To bear it with me through the stormy night:
And, as before, it shone without dismay;
Albeit putting forth a fainter light.

When to the dwelling of my Love I came,
I went into the orchard quietly;
And left the Glow-worm, blessing it by name,
Laid safely by itself, beneath a tree.

The whole next day, I hoped, and hoped with fear;
At night the Glow-worm shone beneath the tree;
I led my Lucy to the spot, "Look here,"
Oh! joy it was for her, and joy for me!

William Wordsworth

To -

Let other bards of angels sing,
Bright suns without a spot;
But thou art no such perfect thing:
Rejoice that thou art not!

Heed not tho' none should call thee fair:
So, Mary, let it be
If naught in loveliness compare
With what thou art to me.

True beauty dwells in deep retreats,
Whose veil is unremoved
Till heart with heart in concord beats,
And the lover is beloved.

William Wordsworth

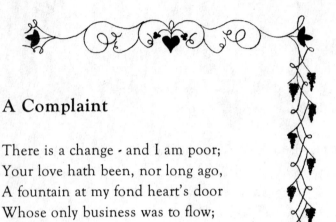

A Complaint

There is a change - and I am poor;
Your love hath been, nor long ago,
A fountain at my fond heart's door
Whose only business was to flow;
And flow it did: not taking heed
Of its own bounty, or my need.

What happy moments did I count!
Blest was I then all bliss above!
Now, for that consecrated fount
Of murmuring, sparkling, living love,
What have I? shall I dare to tell?
A comfortless and hidden well.

A well of love - it may be deep -
I trust it is, and never dry:
What matter? if the waters sleep
In silence and obscurity.
- Such change, and at the very door
Of my fond heart, hath made me poor.

William Wordsworth

Surprised By Joy

Surprised by joy - impatient as the wind
I turned to share the transport - Oh! with whom
But thee, deep buried in the silent tomb,
That spot which no vicissitude can find?
Love, faithful love, recalled thee to my mind -
But how could I forget thee? Through what power,
Even for the least division of an hour,
Have I been so beguiled as to be blind
To my most grievous loss! - That thought's return
Was the worst pang that sorrow ever bore,
Save one, one only, when I stood forlorn,
Knowing my heart's best treasure was no more;
That neither present time, nor years unborn
Could to my sight that heavenly face restore.

William Wordsworth

Remembrance

They flee from me that sometime did me seek
With naked foot stalking in my chamber.
I have seen them gentle, tame and meek,
That now are wild and do not remember
That sometime they put themself in danger
To take bread at my hand; and now they range,
Busily seeking with a continual change.

Thanked be fortune, it hath been otherwise
Twenty times better; but once in special,
In thin array after a pleasant guise,
When her loose gown from her shoulders did fall,
And she me caught in her arms long and small;
Therewithal sweetly did me kiss,
And softly said, dear heart, how like you this?

It was no dream: I lay broad waking,
But all is turned through my gentleness
Into a strange fashion of forsaking;
And I have leave to go of her goodness,
And she also to use newfangleness.
But since that I so kindly am served,
I would fain know what she hath deserved.

Sir Thomas Wyatt

Behold, Love, Thy Power

Behold, love, thy power how she despiseth!
My great pain how little she regardeth!
The holy oath, whereof she taketh no cure,
Broken she hath; and yet she bideth sure
Right at her ease and little she dreadeth.
Weaponed thou art, and she unarmed sitteth;
To the disdainful her life she leadeth,
To me spiteful without cause or measure,
    Behold, love.

I am in hold: if pity thee moveth,
Go bend thy bow, that stony hearts breaketh,
And with some stroke revenge the displeasure
Of thee and him, that sorrow doth endure,
And, as his lord, the lowly entreateth.
    Behold, love.

Sir Thomas Wyatt

A Renouncing Of Love

Farewell, love, and all thy laws forever:
Thy baited hooks shall tangle me no more;
Senec and Plato call me from thy lore,
To perfect wealth my wit for to endeavor.
In blind error when I did persever,
Thy sharp repulse, that pricketh ay so sore,
Hath taught me to set in trifles no store,
And scape forth, since liberty is lever.
Therefore, farewell: go trouble younger hearts,
And in me claim no more authority;
With idle youth go use thy property,
And thereon spend thy many brittle darts;
For hitherto though I have lost all my time,
Me lusteth no longer rotten boughs to climb.

Sir Thomas Wyatt

What Should I Say

What should I say
Since faith is dead,
And truth alway
From you is fled?
Should I be led
With doubleness!
Nay, nay, mistress!

I promised you
And you promised me
To be as true
As I would be;
But since I see
Your double heart,
Farewell my part!

For though to take
It is not my mind
But to forsake -
I am not blind -
And as I find
So will I trust.
Farewell, unjust!

Can ye say nay?
But you said
That I alway
Should be obeyed;
And thus betrayed
Or that I wist -
Farewell, unkissed!

Sir Thomas Wyatt

A Drinking Song

Wine comes in at the mouth
And love comes in at the eye;
That's all we know for truth
Before we grow old and die.
I lift the glass to my mouth,
I look at you, and I sigh.

W.B. Yeats

Brown Penny

I whispered, 'I am too young,'
And then, 'I am old enough';
Wherefore I threw a penny
To find out if I might love,
'Go and love, go and love, young man,
If the lady be young and fair.'
Ah, penny, brown penny, brown penny,
I am looped in the loops of her hair.

O love is the crooked thing
There is nobody wise enough
To find out all that is in it,
For he would be thinking of love
Till the stars had run away
And the shadows eaten the moon.
Ah, penny, brown penny, brown penny,
One cannot begin it too soon.

W.B. Yeats

To An Isle In The Water

Shy one, shy one,
Shy one of my heart.
She moves in the firelight
Pensively apart.

She carries in the dishes,
And lays them in a row.
To an isle in the water
With her would I go.

She carries in the candles,
And lights the curtained room.
Shy in the doorway
And shy in the gloom;

And shy as a rabbit,
Helpful and shy.
To an isle in the water
With her would I fly.

W. B. Yeats

The Pity Of Love

A pity beyond all telling
Is hid in the heart of love:
The folk who are buying and selling;
The clouds on their journey above;
The cold wet winds ever blowing;
And the shadowy hazel grove
Where mouse-grey waters are flowing
Threaten the head that I love.

W. B. Yeats

He Bids His Beloved Be At Peace

I hear the Shadowy Horses, their long manes a-shake,
Their hoofs heavy with tumult, their eyes glimmering
  white;
The North unfolds above them clinging, creeping
  night,
The East her hidden joy before the morning break,
The West weeps in pale dew and sighs passing away,
The South is pouring down roses of crimson fire:
O vanity of Sleep, Hope, Dream, endless Desire,
The Horses of Disaster plunge in the heavy clay:
Beloved, let your eyes half close, and your heartbeat
Over my heart, and your hair fall over my breast,
Drowning love's lonely hour in deep twilight of rest,
And hiding their tossing manes and their tumultuous
  feet.

W. B. Yeats

He Wishes His Beloved Were Dead

Were you but lying cold and dead,
And lights were paling out of the West,
You would come hither, and bend your head,
And I would lay my head on your breast;
And you would murmur tender words,
Forgiving me, because you were dead:
Nor would you rise and hasten away,
Though you have the will of the wild birds,
But know your hair was bound and wound
About the stars and moon and sun:
O would beloved that you lay
Under the dock-leaves in the ground,
While lights were paling one by one.

W. B. Yeats

No Second Troy

Why should I blame her that she filled my days
With misery, or that she would of late
Have taught to ignorant men most violent ways,
Or hurled the little streets upon the great,
Had they but courage equal to desire?
What could have made her peaceful with a mind
That nobleness made simple as a fire,
With beauty like a tightened bow, a kind
That is not natural in an age like this,
Being high and solitary and most stern?
Why what could she have done being what she is?
Was there another Troy for her to burn?

W. B. Yeats

When You Are Old

When you are old and grey and full of sleep,
And nodding by the fire, take down this book,
And slowly read, and dream of the soft look
Your eyes had once, and of their shadows deep;

How many loved your moments of glad grace,
And loved your beauty with love false or true;
But one man loved the pilgrim soul in you,
And loved the sorrows of your changing face.

And bending down beside the glowing bars
Murmur, a little sadly, how Love fled
And paced upon the mountains overhead
And hid his face amid a crowd of stars.

W. B. Yeats

Index of TITLES and First Lines